# CONVEYANCING 1999

# CONVEYANCING 1999

KENNETH G. C. REID WS

Professor of Property Law in the University of Edinburgh

and

GEORGE L. GRETTON WS

Lord President Reid Professor of Law in the University of Edinburgh

T&T CLARK
EDINBURGH
2000

T&T CLARK LTD
59 GEORGE STREET
EDINBURGH EH2 2LQ
SCOTLAND

www.tandtclark.co.uk

First published 2000

ISBN 0 567 00564 X

British Library Cataloguing-in-Publication Data.
A catalogue record for this book is available from the British Library.

Typeset by Waverley Typesetters, Galashiels
Printed and bound in Great Britain by Bell & Bain Ltd, Glasgow

# CONTENTS

# PREFACE

For many years we have been giving an annual update lecture on conveyancing. The present volume is a revised version of the lecture given (in Edinburgh, Glasgow, Oban, Inverness, Aberdeen and Perth) in January and February 2000, and dealing with the year 1999. It is intended as the first of a projected series of annual surveys on conveyancing.

The volume is divided into four parts:

(I) The cases.

(II) The statutory developments.

(III) Other material of interest to conveyancers.

(IV) Detailed commentary on selected issues arising from the first three parts.

The annual lectures concentrate on a calendar year, but in practice this has to be inexact. Cases are by no means always reported in the year in which they were decided, so the haul for a given year includes both cases decided but not yet reported and earlier cases reported for the first time. (In 1999 a decision made in 1930 was reported for the first time: *Aberdeenshire County Council* v *Lord Glentanar* 1999 SLT 1456.) Moreover, we finalise matters not as at 31 December but in the course of January.

This volume is based on the lecture as given, and does not attempt to cover cases decided in recent weeks, such as *Optical Express (Gyle Ltd)* v *Marks & Spencer plc* (Outer House, 8 February 2000), or *Halifax plc* v *Gorman's Tr* (Outer House, 18 February 2000). Such cases will be covered in next year's volume. However, we have made one exception, namely the decision of the Inner House in *M R S Hamilton Ltd* v *Keeper of the Registers of Scotland* on 25 January 2000 reported at 2000 SLT 352. (We will also cover it next year.)

We do not seek to cover agricultural holdings, crofting, public sector tenancies (except the right-to-buy legislation), compulsory purchase or planning law. Otherwise our coverage is intended to be complete.

Finally, it is necessary to say that the text here presented has been prepared rapidly, and therefore without that opportunity for prolonged study which is a prerequisite for a fully polished work. It is commonly said that no text can be said to represent the final views of a living author; if so, the present volume is very much an example of that proposition.

*Kenneth G. C. Reid*
*George L. Gretton*
*March 2000*

# TABLE OF CASES

# TABLE OF STATUTES

# TABLE OF STATUTORY INSTRUMENTS

# PART I

PART I

# CASES

## MISSIVES

### (1) Palmer v Forsyth 1999 SLT (Sh Ct) 93

In terms of missives there was a right to resile if the 'title deeds' were not 'entirely satisfactory' to the purchasers, as to which the purchasers were to be the 'sole judge'. The purchasers resiled, but their decision was challenged. **Held**: (a) There was no obligation to give reasons for resiling. (b) There was an implied term that, in exercising their right to resile, the purchasers should act reasonably, and not arbitrarily or capriciously. (c) But there were no averments by the seller as to the manner in which the purchasers were alleged to have acted unreasonably. See **Commentary** p 40.

### (2) N J & J Macfarlane (Developments) Ltd v MacSween's Trs 1999 SLT 619 (OH)

**Held**: That the specifications of property and price contained in missives were so indeterminate that the missives were unenforceable.

### (3) Super (Tom) Printing and Supplies Ltd v South Lanarkshire Council 1999 GWD 31–1496 and 38–1854 (OH)

Parties entered into negotiations, the basis of which was that (a) the Council would buy the pursuers' property for £900,000, and (b) the pursuers would buy a retail unit from the Council. Some months after the preliminary agreement was reached, the terms were varied so as to allow for compensation for delay by the Council in providing the new unit. A dispute then arose as to whether there was a contract at all. There was no formal written contract. There was also a question as to whether the Council's officials had any authority to enter into such a contract. The pursuers argued that there had been actings under s 1(3) and (4) of the Requirements of Writing (Scotland) Act 1995, particularly in relation to preparations for the new retail unit. They sought declarator that there was a contract. **Held**: Action dismissed. The actings must be referable to the contract as varied, but here most related to the period prior to the variation, and those which occurred subsequently were equivocal, and could equally be attributed to the contract in its original state.

#### (4) Homecare Contracts (Scotland) Ltd v Scottish Midland Co-operative Society Ltd 1999 GWD 23–1111 (Sh Ct)

Subjects of sale were damaged after conclusion of missives but before settlement. On the face of it, the missives denied a claim if the purchasers duly settled the transaction, as they had here. None the less, in a claim for damages proof was allowed. See **Commentary** p 39.

[Another aspect of this case is digested at (11).]

#### (5) Hamilton v Rodwell (No 2) 1999 GWD 35–1706 (OH)

When a conveyancing transaction settled a retention of £10,500 was made, in terms of the missives, and placed on joint deposit receipt for repairs required in respect of statutory repairs notices. The missives took the seller bound to pay for the repairs, but they were also subject to a two-year non-supersession clause. The repairs were eventually completed, but the seller did not pay. Under the relevant legislation the buyers were liable to the local authority for the cost. The money remained on deposit receipt. Eventually the buyers raised this action to try to uplift the deposit receipt to pay for the repairs.

Their first attempt (reported at 1998 SCLR 418) failed. This was because (a) the whole deposit receipt arrangement was contained in the missives (b) as was the seller's obligation to pay, but (c) two years having expired, the missives were no longer enforceable.

The buyers amended and made a second attempt. This time their argument focused on the terms of the disposition. This declared that the transfer was in consideration of the price of £90,000 (being the full consideration) 'of which sum I hereby acknowledge receipt'. But if, or so it was argued, the seller had (as the disposition said) *already* received the full purchase price, it followed that the money still held on deposit receipt belonged to the buyers and should be paid to them. This not very strong argument was rejected by the court. The seller had not in fact received the full consideration, unless one were to include the money on deposit receipt. Viewed in this way, the terms of the discharge in the disposition actually indicated that the money placed on deposit receipt was part of the consideration (as indeed it was), and hence 'belonged' to the seller.

The case seems to leave the deposit receipt in limbo. For whilst the supersession of the missives meant that the buyers could not claim the deposit receipt, it is difficult to see how the seller could claim it either, without himself relying on the missives. The case illustrates the dangers of a too-short cut-off period, and also of 'D/R settlements'.

#### (6) Smith v Lindsay & Kirk 2000 SLT 287 (IH)

Missives contained (a) the usual obligation to deliver a disposition and (b) an obligation on the seller to convert a steading building on the land into a dwellinghouse. The seller performed (a) but not (b). There was a two-year non-supersession clause, but the purchaser did not raise an action of damages within this period. When the purchaser sued his solicitor for failing to raise the action timeously, it was argued for the solicitor that the non-supersession clause did not prevent an action of *damages* outwith the two-year period. This argument was rejected. See **Commentary** p 41.

This reverses the decision of the Lord Ordinary reported at 1998 SLT 1096, 1998 SCLR 572.

### (7) Keenan v Aberdeen Slating Co 2000 SC 81 (IH)

The pursuer, who operated a snooker and leisure club at 98–108 John Street Aberdeen, concluded missives to buy adjacent property. Whilst entry and vacant possession was to be on 28 March 1995, settlement (including payment of the price) was to be postponed by a year, to 29 February 1996. During the interim the pursuer was to pay interest on the price. Interest was duly paid, but the defenders were in default on their contractual obligations by failing to give full vacant possession during the gap year prior to settlement. This meant that the pursuer could not use the property, as he intended, as an extension to his existing premises. When the date for settlement came, a dispute arose as to how much should be paid. The defenders insisted on the full price. The pursuer insisted on deducting the instalments of interest already paid. **Held**: The full price was due. (In the end, this was conceded by counsel for the pursuer.) For the period that the defenders were in default, it would have been open to the pursuer to withhold performance, by not paying interest. He chose not to adopt this course. Now that performance was finally being offered, he must in turn perform by tendering the full purchase price. Any loss suffered as a result of the defenders' breach could only be settled by a claim for damages (a claim was being made as part of the same action), but, since the claim was necessarily illiquid, it could not be set off against the liability for the price.

## OPTIONS

### (8) Robertson v Secretary of State for Scotland
### 1999 GWD 26–1251 (Sh Ct)

The defender was under an obligation to offer to the pursuer a former hospital (Bridge of Earn Hospital) at a price reflecting current market value. An offer was made based on a figure produced by the district valuer. This was not ordinary open market value but rather a 'best price' value, which took into account any bid made by a purchaser with a special interest, and was accordingly higher. **Held**: (a) 'best price' was not the appropriate basis of valuation, (b) in any event the valuation had failed to take sufficient account of (i) the cost and removal of asbestos and (ii) a real burden to maintain and keep clear two pipes deep underground, and (c) a proper determination of value required negotiation and discussion in advance.

# LAW OF THE TENEMENT

### (9) Richardson v Quercus Ltd 1999 SC 278, 1999 SLT 596 (IH)

The owner of two upper flats (at 16 Howe Street, Edinburgh) was awarded damages for repairs made necessary by work carried out by the owners of a lower flat, including removal of a load-bearing wall. The lower owner conceded liability in principle, and the present litigation was concerned with quantum, and with the argument that the claim had prescribed negatively. At first instance (reported at 1997 GWD 17–804) it was held that the quinquennial prescription was prevented from operating by the continuing correspondence between the parties in which liability was admitted. Accordingly, the upper owner was awarded £44,865.85 for the repairs to his property, plus £2,000 for the inconvenience of having to move out. The lower owner appealed against the decision on prescription, but the decision was upheld.

### (10) Hamilton v Wahla 1999 GWD 25–1217 (Sh Ct)

This case was similar to Case (9) above. It was an action by the owner of a first floor flat against the tenant of the shop beneath for damage caused by alterations to the shop, including the removal of walls. The upper owner sued both on the basis of nuisance and also for vicarious liability in negligence (the work actually having been carried out by contractors). The defender argued that since he was a mere tenant, and since he had given up occupation during the currency of the works, he had only a transient involvement during the construction. **Held**: Damages were awarded. The defender's involvement was not merely transient. It was settled that in instructing others to carry out works, there could be liability for risks arising from such instructions, even if not done under the defender's close direction.

# COMMON PROPERTY

### (11) Homecare Contracts (Scotland) Ltd v Scottish Midland Co-operative Society Ltd 1999 GWD 23–1111 (Sh Ct)

This case concerned a two-flat tenement. The harling of one of the walls, which was owned in common, was defective. One co-owner instructed the repair without consulting the other. Now he sought reimbursement of half of the cost, on the basis that this was a 'necessary' repair and hence could be carried out unilaterally. It was argued for the other co-owner that a repair was 'necessary' only (a) in cases of emergency or (b) if the other owner, on being consulted, refused to play any part in the repair. But otherwise it would be the duty of an owner to involve the other owner. He could not simply go ahead on his own initiative, and then pass the bill over for payment. **Held**: Proof was allowed. The provisional view expressed was that there was no obligation to consult the other owner. (We would observe that the same conclusion had been reached more than 100 years ago in *Rennie* v *McGill* (1885) 1 Sh Ct Rep 158, a case not cited by the court.)

[Another aspect of this case is digested at (4).]

### (12) Johnston v Johnston 1999 GWD 7–347 (OH)

This was a fact-specific case. It was an action of division or sale of agricultural land in which the question of whether division, and if so how, was remitted to a reporter. Both parties challenged certain aspects of the resulting report. Some of the complaints were rejected by the court but others were judged worthy of being remitted back to the reporter.

### (13) Bush v Bush 2000 SLT (Sh Ct) 22

An unmarried couple were co-owners of a house. On splitting up, they entered into an agreement whereby the woman was to convey her half share to the man in exchange for £10,000. Neither side of the bargain seems to have been implemented, though the woman raised an action for the price. No money having been recovered, the woman then raised this action for division and sale. The man argued that an action of division and sale was excluded by the contract to transfer the half share, or, alternatively, by personal bar. **Held**: The defences were repelled. There was an absolute right to division and sale and, whilst this could be excluded by contract, there was no evidence that this had been done in the present case. The fact that there was also a separate contractual remedy did not take away the right to division and sale.

## STATUTORY NOTICES

### (14) City of Edinburgh Council v Aslam 1999 Hous LR 124 (Sh Ct)

The Council served a notice under s 13 of the Building (Scotland) Act 1959. Subsequently, the Council itself carried out the required works. One of those on whom the notice was served refused to pay his share of the costs, arguing that his premises formed part of a separate building. A proof was allowed. The case contains some discussion of the respective roles of judicial review and appeal.

## SERVITUDES AND RIGHTS OF WAY

### (15) Wimpey Homes Holdings Ltd v Collins 1999 SLT (Sh Ct) 16

A servitude was reserved over a road. The road was potentially 37 feet in width but, at the time of the reservation, only around 18 feet was in use, the rest being trees and hedges. The dominant proprietors cleared the remaining width of the road and levelled and resurfaced it. The servient proprietors challenged this, seeking interdict and damages. **Held**: Since the servitude extended over the full width of the road, the dominant proprietors had acted within their rights.

### (16) Axis West Developments Ltd v Chartwell 1999 SLT 1416 (HL)

This was a case on the interpretation of servitudes. See **Commentary** p 50. It affirms the decision of the First Division reported at 1998 GWD 13–674.

### (17) Rubislaw Land Co Ltd v Aberdeen Construction Group Ltd
### 1999 GWD 14–647 (OH)

Originally the defenders owned both Rubislaw Quarry (no longer worked) and also adjacent ground, known as the 'Campus Site'. By a deed of conditions it was provided that the owners of the Quarry should have a right of access over a road running round its perimeter (and over the Campus Site), but subject to a number of conditions. These included a right by the owners of the Campus Site to alter the location of the road. Subsequently, there was a disposition to the pursuers of the Quarry by the then owners, a subsidiary of the defenders. Whilst this granted an unqualified servitude over the road, the deed of conditions was also incorporated by reference. The pursuers sought a declarator of unqualified access rights. The defenders resisted. They argued (a) that the pursuers could only take access to the road at the single point at which this was done at the time when the deed of conditions was granted, (b) that in any event the road was not usually contiguous to the pursuers' boundary, and where it was not they had no right to take access at that point (since they had no rights over the defenders' land apart from the road), and (c) that the servitude right was qualified by the terms of the deed of conditions. **Held**: Proof was allowed, though (c) in particular seemed to be correct.

The eventual proof may give rise to some interesting law, but two points may be mentioned for the moment. First, since the granters of the pursuers' disposition did not own the road, it is not clear how they could grant a servitude over it. In general, only the owner of property can grant a servitude (or other subordinate real right) over it. (The granters of the pursuers' disposition could, of course, transmit the benefit of any such servitude as had been previously created by the deed of conditions.)

Second, the pursuers founded on *Kildrummy (Jersey) Ltd v IRC* 1991 SC 1 to argue that the deed of conditions was a nullity, since a person cannot contract with himself. This argument was rejected without much difficulty on the basis of the special statutory regime for deeds of conditions. But Lord Penrose also threw doubt on *Kildrummy* itself, remarking that 'there would be an interesting issue for a higher court whether *Kildrummy (Jersey)* was correctly decided, since the successful argument there proceeded largely on English authority'. It should also be noted that in an English case in 1999 the House of Lords has not followed *Kildrummy* (*Ingram* v *Inland Revenue* [1999] 1 All ER 297). We also have grave doubts as to the correctness of the decision in *Kildrummy*.

### (18) Cloy v T M Adams & Sons 1999 GWD 19–908 (Sh Ct)

If the exercise of a servitude causes danger, it ceases to be lawful. See **Commentary** p 49.

### (19) Inverness Seafield Development Co Ltd v Mackintosh 1999 GWD 31–1497 (OH)

Here there was an option to buy land, or part of land. Eventually the option was exercised, but in relation to part of the land only. This left the remaining part landlocked. Accordingly, when the sellers came to draft a disposition they sought to include an express reservation of a servitude in their favour. This was resisted by purchasers. **Held**: The servitude should be included. This was a servitude of necessity, implied into the original contract. See **Commentary** p 48. The action was dismissed.

The action in fact took the form—most unusually—of an action for adjudication. The purchasers were seeking to avoid being handed a disposition in terms they did not like by obtaining instead a judicial conveyance. It is not clear why the more usual route of an action seeking specific implement was not adopted.

### (20) Aberdeenshire County Council v Lord Glentanar 1999 SLT 1456 (OH)

This, though the last Court of Session case to be reported by *Scots Law Times* in the millennium just ended, actually dates from 5 December 1930. The case is, however, discussed at para 21–07 of D J Cusine and R R M Paisley, *Servitudes and Rights of Way*. The issue before the court was whether, in the prescriptive acquisition of a public right of way, use by bicycle could establish a general right of vehicular use. The answer given by Lord Mackay was negative. 'The expression "vehicle" . . . as used in right of way cases, is in my opinion apt to express a sharp distinction between machines for carrying passengers over the country by some sort of motive power which precludes them from using their own legs for the purpose, and, on the other hand, any form of contrivance, such as a skate or roller skate or snowshoe, which merely facilitates the use of the individual's own muscle to cover ground more quickly. Accordingly, I take the view that the pedal cycle is only an aid to pedestrianism.'

The decision indicates that where there is a pedestrian right of way it is also available to cyclists. The implications of that will need to be considered by local authorities and others. It is possible that the same rule would apply in relation to *servitudes* of way established by prescription.

## REAL BURDENS

### (21) Heritage Fisheries Ltd v Duke of Roxburghe 1999 GWD 24–1161 (IH)

This case turned on the interpretation of a maintenance clause in a deed of conditions. See **Commentary** p 57.

### (22) Marsden v Craighelen Lawn Tennis and Squash Club
### 1999 GWD 37–1820 (Sh Ct)

A 1927 disposition contained a prohibition on using property other than as tennis courts. Certain neighbours raised an action to prevent contravention of this prohibition. **Held**: (a) the prohibition was not a real burden; (b) in any event, the pursuers had no title to enforce under the rule in *J A Mactaggart & Co v Harrower* (1906) 8 F 1101, in the absence of an express assignation; (c) in any event, there was no interest to enforce. See **Commentary** p 59.

# VARIATION AND DISCHARGE
# OF LAND OBLIGATIONS

### (23) Anderson v Trotter 1999 SLT 442 (IH)

Number 295 Lanark Road, Edinburgh (a dwellinghouse in a small housing development of one acre) was converted into a nursery with a flat above. At first, planning permission was given only for a year, but thereafter unrestricted permission was given. The nursery duly opened. But use in this way was contrary to a feudal real burden imposed in 1901 on the whole acre. The burden was mutually enforceable by the other owners within this area. They opposed the use as a nursery. When the owners of number 295 applied for a variation of the burden, this was refused.

The application was made under grounds (a) and (c) of s 1(3) of the 1970 Act. So far as ground (a) ('changes in the character of the land ... or of the neighbourhood') is concerned, the Tribunal took the view that 'neighbourhood' in this context meant, not Lanark Road (which had plainly changed into a very busy road) but the quiet one-acre development, of which number 295 formed part.

In relation to ground (c) (*ie* a burden which 'impedes some reasonable use') the Tribunal decided that, taking into account the increased traffic and increased noise from the small suburban garden, the use was not reasonable. The Tribunal refused to give weight to the grant of unrestricted planning permission, on the basis that this was obtained only after the burden had been breached and so would not have been available to the applicants if (as ought to have happened) they had applied to the Tribunal earlier.

The Tribunal also expressed the view that it should be slow to exercise its power to vary what was, in effect, a mutual contract where that would involve a first departure from that contract. Otherwise this might be the thin edge of the wedge.

On appeal, the Second Division upheld the approach taken by the Tribunal.

# WARRANDICE

## (24)  Baird v Drumpellier & Mount Vernon Estates Ltd
## 2000 SC 103 (OH)

Missives were concluded for the sale of a plot of land at Carrick Drive, Mount Vernon, Glasgow, for £10,000. There had been some doubt as to whether the sellers owned the land. Whether for that, or for some other, reason the missives did not contain the usual clause about good and marketable title. However, the disposition, when granted, did contain a grant of absolute warrandice. In the event, the disposition was rejected by the Keeper on the basis that a competing title existed. The buyer then sued in warrandice. **Held**: Proof on quantum was allowed. The sellers' counterclaim to have the disposition rectified, so as to substitute a grant of simple warrandice, was rejected.

Three points may be mentioned. (1) The court, rightly, made it clear that, even without an express stipulation in missives for good and marketable title, there is an implied term to the same effect. (2) There appears to have been no mention of 'judicial eviction', yet that is a pre-requisite of a claim in warrandice under a disposition. (3) Finally, a practical point. It sometimes happens that a seller agrees to take title as it stands (perhaps in relation to the whole property or perhaps in relation only to part), and the missives are framed to reflect this agreement. But then, when the disposition comes to be granted, the dead hand of words of style takes over, and absolute warrandice is granted. (We offer this as a general observation and not as an interpretation of this particular case.)

# EXECUTION OF DEEDS

## (25)  Forsyth v Royal Bank of Scotland plc 2000 SCLR 61 (OH)

The case turned on the law on execution as it stood before the Requirements of Writing (Scotland) Act 1995. A standard security was granted by a husband and wife in favour of a bank, and was duly registered in the Register of Sasines. But whilst the wife had duly signed, the two witnesses had neither seen her sign nor heard her acknowledge her signature. In principle, this was fatal to validity. However, it was argued that since (a) the wife did actually sign, (b) although there may have been some misrepresentation by her husband, she did at least know that the security was a formality relating to the overdraft for her husband's business and (c) the bank relied on the security in making advances to the business, therefore the defect was cured by *rei interventus*. **Held**: This was a relevant case of *rei interventus*. (The doctrine is quite well established in this kind of context: see, *eg Boyd* v *Shaw* 1927 SC 414.)

Note that under current law execution by the granter is sufficient, and a deed cannot be reduced merely on the ground that the witness neither saw the granter sign nor heard her acknowledge her signature.

[Another aspect of this decision is digested at (57).]

## (26) Young v Archibald 1999 GWD 4–205 (OH)

This was a rather similar case. A house at 24 Cathcart Place, Edinburgh, was owned in common by Michael Young and Muriel Archibald. What bore to be a valid disposition of Young's half share was granted to Archibald and duly recorded in the Sasine Register. But Young thereafter denied that the signature was his, and he also denied that the two witnesses to the deed actually saw him sign or heard him acknowledge his signature. Subsequently, Archibald sold to Rehka Begum, who granted a standard security to the Halifax. Neither Begum nor the Halifax knew of the defect in the execution of the original disposition. Young sought reduction of the original disposition. The defect in the witnessing was a matter of concession, but it was found, after proof, that Young had indeed signed. The court granted absolvitor.

The legal basis of the decision is not clear. Under the law as it was before the Requirements of Writing (Scotland) Act 1995 a disposition which has not been properly witnessed is void, unless there is *rei interventus* or homologation. Neither seems to have been pled. And nor is there much sign of *rei interventus* in respect of Archibald. (The purchase by Begum and the loan by the Halifax might, however, be in a different position.)

One aspect of the case deserves further comment. Young had sought to show that his signature had been forged. In the event, he failed. But the court indicated that, even if he had been successful, it would not have granted a reduction because of the effect on Begum and the Halifax. Instead, there would have been an award of damages against Archibald. But this approach seems, with respect, to involve a misapprehension of the effect of forgery in terms of property law and conveyancing. No rights can pass under a forged disposition. So Young would have remained the owner, *whether a reduction was granted or not*. (In the case of a void deed, a reduction is merely declaratory in effect.) And if Young had still owned, it would follow that ownership could not have been acquired by Begum from Archibald: *nemo plus juris ad alium transferre potest quam ipse haberet*. Thus, even if reduction were refused and damages awarded, Young would remain the owner of a half share. (These comments are based on the fact that the property in question was in the Sasine Register. Had the property been in the Land Register the correct analysis would have been different. For a parallel case in the Land Register see *Kaur* v *Singh* 1998 SCLR 849, 1999 SC 180.)

# REGISTRATION OF TITLE

## (27) Keeper of the Registers of Scotland v M R S Hamilton Ltd
### 1999 SC 116, 1999 SLT 855 (IH)

Following success before the Lands Tribunal, Hamilton sought expenses under s 13 of the Land Registration (Scotland) Act 1979 (which provides for reimbursement of expenses incurred in pursuing a prima facie well-founded claim under s 12, whether successful or not). The Keeper rejected this as premature on the basis that an appeal was pending, and the Inner House declined to interfere with this decision.

### (28)  M R S Hamilton Ltd v Keeper of the Registers of Scotland (No 1)
### 1999 SLT 829 (OH)

In 1986 title to a 999-year lease was registered in the Land Register. By mistake, additional land from the estate was included in the title plan. (This additional land had in fact been possessed by the tenants.) When M R S Hamilton Ltd acquired the *dominium utile* of the estate in 1994 it sought, and was refused, rectification. (The Keeper could not rectify because there was a proprietor in possession, and indemnity had not been excluded.) M R S Hamilton Ltd now sought payment of indemnity.

M R S Hamilton Ltd's principal case was a direct claim for indemnity. It had suffered loss. Hence, indemnity was payable. The Keeper defended on the basis that the proper claimant should be the owner of the estate in 1986, at the time when the mistake was made. Lord Hamilton held the claim to be relevant. However, the Keeper was allowed proof on M R S Hamilton Ltd's state of knowledge at the time of purchase, the implication being that a person who buys with his eyes open has suffered no loss.

Proof was also allowed on the question of whether the 1986 owner had been the author of his own (and subsequent owners') misfortunes by allowing the tenant to possess too much and so misleading the Keeper when it came to first registration. The relevance of this is that indemnity is not paid (or is restricted) if the loss was caused wholly (or in part) by the fraudulent or careless act of the claimant: see s 12(3)(n) and 13(4) of the 1979 Act.

M R S Hamilton Ltd also had a claim in the alternative, as assignee of the 1986 estate owner. This claim was also held to be relevant (in the event that the first claim failed), although, in view of the apparent ignorance of the then owner, and of the person who purchased from that owner, there might be difficulty in showing loss. Lord Hamilton approved the view expressed by the Lands Tribunal in the earlier case (a) that s 12(1)(d) of the 1979 Act should be widely interpreted, (b) that claims for indemnity are freely assignable, and (c) that they prescribe only after 20 years.

### (29)  M R S Hamilton Ltd v Keeper of the Registers of Scotland (No 2)
### 1999 SLT 840 (OH)

This was an expenses claim made in respect of the immediately preceding case. The argument that s 13(1) of the 1979 Act placed liability on the Keeper only in respect of *extra*-judicial expenses was rejected. Expenses were awarded on a party-and-party basis, reserving any claim for additional expenditure under s 13(1).

### (30)  Short's Tr v Chung (No 2) 1999 SLT 751 (IH)

Alexander Short owned two flats at 62 Great George Street, Glasgow. He disponed them to Shek Chung. Short was insolvent at the time and this was a gratuitous alienation. Chung then gave the properties to Tai Lee Chung, his wife. Tai Lee Chung was entered as proprietor in the Land Register. Short was then sequestrated.

Litigations of various kinds followed. In this litigation Short's trustee in sequestration sought, and was granted, a decree ordaining Tai Lee Chung to grant a
disposition of the properties to the trustee.

This affirms the decision of the Lord Ordinary reported at 1997 SCLR 1181,
1998 SC 105, 1998 SLT 200. See **Commentary** p 69.

### (31)  Dougbar Properties Ltd v Keeper of the Registers of Scotland
### 1999 SC 513, 1999 SCLR 458 (OH)

The title sheet to a long lease mistakenly included a right to park in an adjacent
car park, which was part of a different property, though leased from the same
landlord. Later the lease was assigned. The assignees knew at the time of the
purchase that the title sheet was erroneous on this point. Subsequently, the Keeper
rectified the Register by removing the right of car-parking. (The assignees were
not in 'possession' of this right and so rectification was not barred by the 'proprietor
in possession' rule.) The assignees claimed indemnity from the Keeper, on the
ground that they had been prejudiced by the rectification. **Held**: In principle
indemnity was payable. See **Commentary** p 71.

### (32)  Stevenson-Hamilton's Exrs v McStay
### 1999 SLT 1175, 1999 SCLR 488 (OH)

The defenders were registered in the Land Register as owners of property at
81 Clyde Street, Carluke. The pursuers claimed that the property had previously
been theirs, and that the disposition presented by the defenders was *a non
domino*. Accordingly, they sought reduction of the disposition, and an order for
rectification, on the basis that the defenders were either fraudulent or careless
within s 9(3)(a)(iii) of the Land Registration (Scotland) Act 1979. The stage of the
litigation reported here was concerned with a side issue. The pursuers sought
damages from the defenders for physical injury caused to the property. This was
resisted on the basis that, at the time of the injury, the defenders were registered
owners, and so if they were damaging anything they were only damaging their
*own* property. Furthermore, they argued, the position would not be changed
even if the pursuers succeeded in their main action, because the effect of
rectification would not be retrospective. This defence was accepted by the court.
See **Commentary** p 68.

### (33)  Wilson v Keeper of the Registers of Scotland 2000 SLT 267,
### 1999 SCLR 872 (IH)

The case involved complex facts, not all of which were properly before the court,
and not all of which are fully explained in the judgment. The essence seems to
be the following. In 1965 the Clyde Port Authority took title to Greenock Harbour.
This seems to have been partly under the Clyde Port Authority Order Confirmation
Act 1965 and partly by a statutory conveyance (*ie* a conveyance in the form of
Sched A to the Land Clauses Consolidation (Scotland) Act 1845). They possessed
peacefully until 1987, when they sold the Harbour to the Scottish Development

Agency (now Scottish Enterprise). The sale induced first registration in the Land Register, and the SDA (now Scottish Enterprise) were duly entered in the Land Register as owners.

Much later, the position of Scottish Enterprise was challenged by some members of the community of Inverclyde (the appellants). They argued (a) that part of the Harbour had been conveyed to the Magistrates of Greenock in 1772 in trust for the people of Greenock (of which the appellants were said to be representatives), (b) that that part had never been conveyed away, (c) that any purported conveyance to the SDA was *a non domino*, (d) that the Land Register was inaccurate to that extent, and (e) that, accordingly, the Register should be rectified to that extent, by substituting as owner Inverclyde Council (as the statutory successors of the original 1772 trustees).

The Keeper refused to rectify. An appeal to the Lands Tribunal against that decision was refused on 29 July 1998. (The decision is by Robin Edwards WS and has not been reported. It is full of interest.) This was a further appeal against that refusal.

**Held**: The appeal was refused. There were three grounds for the refusal. (1) The appellants had no title to sue. The proper person to seek rectification in this case was Inverclyde Council (*ie* the trustees rather than the beneficiaries of the alleged trust). A successful application would make the Council owner. That could only be allowed to occur on the application of the Council itself. The Council did not support the application. Further, the alternative to rectification under the Act was indemnity, and it was clear that only the Council could seek indemnity. (There can be little doubt that this view of matters was sound. If a beneficiary feels that a trustee is failing to protect trust assets, the beneficiary should take the issue up with the trustee, if necessary by litigation.)

(2) It was not clear that the Register was, as a matter of fact, inaccurate. Prescription seemed to have run. And there was the possible argument, not resolved by the case, that a statutory conveyance cures absence of title. The title difficulties had not been properly argued.

(3) Even if the Register were inaccurate, it could not be rectified against Scottish Enterprise, as a proprietor in possession, unless they had been fraudulent or careless. Fraud was not suggested, and no proper arguments had been brought as to carelessness.

See **Commentary** p 67.

### (34)  Kaur v Singh (No 2) 2000 SCLR 187, 1999 Hous LR 76 (OH)

This is the successor to *Kaur* v *Singh* 1998 SCLR 849, 1999 SC 180. The pursuer owned a flat in common with her husband at 3/2, 30 Woodlands Drive, Glasgow. Her husband sold it without telling her, forging her signature. Singh, the purchaser, was entered on the Register as owner, but the Register was inaccurate. At one stage the pursuer's strategy seems to have been to dispossess Singh by force, so that he was no longer a proprietor in possession. Latterly this approach was abandoned, and the pursuer accepted that the Keeper could not rectify the Register against Singh. Instead, she sought payment of indemnity by the Keeper. The current stage of this litigation concerns quantum. (For some of the background to this complex dispute see Professor Gretton's commentary at the end of the 1998 SCLR report.)

It was agreed between the parties that the pursuer's loss was to be measured as at 8 March 1996, being the date that the inaccurate entry on the Register was made. Lord Macfadyen, however, expressly reserved his decision on this point, and there is an obvious argument to the effect that the valuation should be taken as at the date when rectification is refused. Be that as it may, the issue between the parties was a different one. As at 8 March 1996 the flat was valued at £51,000. But until 7 March it had been subject to a secured loan, with the Woolwich, of £41,000. So the pursuer's share of the equity was only £5,000. The pursuer's husband had redeemed the loan as part of the sale.

The pursuer claimed £25,500 (*ie* half the value of the flat). The Keeper was willing to pay only £5,000, on the basis that this was her real loss from the total transaction. **Held**: The amount due by the Keeper was £25,500. The broader circumstances were not relevant. The question was: what loss did the pursuer suffer from the failure to rectify? If the Keeper had duly rectified, the pursuer would have received an unencumbered half share of the flat, worth £25,500. That, therefore, was the extent of her loss for present purposes.

The result looks like a windfall gain for the pursuer. In theory, Mr Kaur could presumably claim from Mrs Kaur one half of the loan of £41,000, which he had paid off to her benefit, *ie* £20,5000. If that were to happen, Mrs Kaur would end up with £25,500 − £20,500 = £5,000. But one suspects that in practice she will end up keeping the extra.

We understand that the decision has been appealed.


# RIGHT-TO-BUY LEGISLATION

## (35) City of Glasgow Council v Peart 1999 Hous LR 117 (OH)

The landlord issued an offer to sell on 30 May 1989, in favour of the tenant and her son-in-law. An acceptance (from the tenant's agents) came back on 26 June 1989, but this was not signed. A properly signed acceptance followed on 28 July 1989. However, between these two dates the tenant had died (on 15 July). The landlord raised an action against the son-in-law (a) to reduce the offer to sell as having been induced by fraud, and (b) to reduce the signed letter of accept-ance as having been too late. No decision was made on the first point (which would have required a proof), but decree was granted on the second. Death terminates agency, and so the solicitors simply could not validly issue the letter of acceptance after the death of their client. One argument for the defender was that the landlord's offer to sell had been issued three weeks late, and that if it had been issued timeously a concluded contract would have been in place before the death of the tenant. This cut no ice with the court. It should be noted that the facts of this case are different from those in *Cooper's Exrs v Edinburgh District Council* 1991 SC(HL) 5, where the tenant died *after* the contract had been concluded.

The decision as to the lapse of authority by death is certainly correct. But the case raises the academic question, of general contractual interest, of whether an executor could validly accept an offer made to the deceased. (This did not in fact happen in the present case.) In theory the answer is probably affirmative, in the absence of *delectus personae*. But in practice the issue is unlikely to arise often, since such an acceptance could presumably be made only by a *confirmed* executor, and by the time an executor has been confirmed an unaccepted offer is unlikely still to be on the table.

### (36)  Souter v Aberdeen City Council, 15 December 1999 (unreported) (IH)

Mrs McDonald was a council tenant at 37B Westburn Road, Aberdeen. She exercised her right to buy, and received a discount of £31,500. The feu disposition in her favour was recorded GRS Aberdeen on 2 March 1994. On 17 March 1994 she granted a trust deed for creditors, duly registered in the Books of Council and Session on 5 May 1994. The trustee did not complete title. The question was whether the trust deed triggered liability to repay the discount in terms of s 72 of the Housing (Scotland) Act 1987. It was held that it did. Lord Gill: 'A disposal under s 72 need not involve a formal conveyance. It is sufficient that the former tenant puts it out of his power to deal with the house as owner.'

The decision may offer local authorities ammunition for various sorts of challenge, not just in cases of trust deeds. For instance, suppose that a purchaser, Janet, is financed by her daughter, Margaret, and they agree in writing that Janet will hold the property in trust for herself in liferent and for Margaret in fee. Arrangements of this sort are not uncommon. Is such an arrangement a 'disposal'? No one knows, but the possibility that it is is strengthened by the new decision.

Two technical footnotes on the case. The first is that it seems to have been a matter of concession that the trust deed was revocable after it was delivered but became irrevocable when it was recorded in the Books of Council and Session. Possibly there were specialities here which gave rise to that result, but if so we do not know what they were. The law is that, in the absence of special circumstances, a trust deed for creditors is irrevocable when it is delivered to and accepted by the trustee. The second technical footnote is that there was some discussion of an old theory that a trust deed for creditors does not transfer legal ownership to the trustee. That doctrine may be right or wrong (we think it wrong). But it was irrelevant to the present case, because the trustee never completed title, and so the question of transfer of legal ownership to him could not arise.

## LEASES

### (37)  City of Aberdeen Council v Clark 1999 SLT 613 (IH)

A 99-year lease was granted in 1970 for rent of £300 per annum. It had a provision for rent review every 21 years. (Those were the days. . . .) The clause read:

Not less than three months prior to the 28th September 1991 and not less than three months prior to the expiry of every period of twenty-one years thereafter during the currency of this Lease or any extension thereof in terms of clause (Sixteenth) hereof, the Corporation or the Tenants may at their discretion, by notice in writing, require that the rent payable by the Tenants in terms hereof, being rent for the ground leased exclusive of any buildings thereon, be re-negotiated or, failing agreement, be determined by an Arbiter to be mutually chosen or, in the event of failure to agree, by an Arbiter to be appointed by the Chairman for the time being of the Scottish Branch of the Royal Institution of Chartered Surveyors.

The tenants argued that the clause was void by reason of uncertainty, relying on *Crawford* v *Bruce* 1992 SLT 524 where a clause reading simply 'with a review of the rent on the expiry of each three year period' was held void for uncertainty. **Held**: that the clause was valid. It was an implied term that a 'fair and reasonable' rent be set.

It is perhaps not easy to reconcile the decision with *Crawford*. In practice, the court was evidently influenced by the fact that in a 99-year lease the absence of a valid review clause would have more serious consequences than it would in a 15-year lease (as in *Crawford*).

### (38)  UCB Bank plc v Hire Foulis Ltd
### 1999 SC 250, 1999 SLT 950, 1999 SCLR 35 (IH)

A landlord went into liquidation. Who was entitled to the rents: (a) the liquidator, or (b) the standard security holder? **Held**: The liquidator. See **Commentary** p 43.

### (39)  Moray Estates Development Co v Butler
### 1999 SLT 1338, 1999 SCLR 447 (OH)

What happens if there is a lease to a partnership, and there is a change in the membership of the partnership? Might that terminate the lease? See **Commentary** p 44.

### (40)  Quarantelli v Forbes 2000 GWD 2–67 (Sh Ct)

Landlords sought to recover possession of property, on two grounds. One was that the tenants were a partnership, and that the partnership had been dissolved. On this see **Commentary** p 44. The other was that an irritancy had been incurred. Decree granted in favour of the pursuers.

### (41)  Minevco Ltd v Barratt Southern Ltd 1999 GWD 5–266 (OH)

A lease provided that the tenants would 'use their best endeavours' to develop the property and also adjacent property, conform to planning permission. Over the years there were various amendments in the lease and also in the planning permissions. The landlords eventually sued for specific implement, which failing damages. Proof before answer allowed. The case is a fact-specific one turning on the correct interpretation of the original agreement, as varied.

### (42) Glasgow City Council v Torrance 1999 GWD 35–1708 (Sh Ct)

A tied house was let to a janitor, the lease to end one month after his retirement. The landlords wrote to the tenant saying that 'you are expected to move ... within three months of your retiral'. **Held**: that this was not effectual as a notice to quit. It did not unequivocally require the tenant to remove, and 'within three months' was too indeterminate. (Notices to quit are easy to get wrong. They require careful drafting.)

### (43) Denovan v Blue Triangle (Glasgow) Housing Association Ltd 1999 Hous LR 97 (Sh Ct)

This and the next case concern the question of whether a provider of hostel accommodation is entitled to insist that a resident leave without prior notice. (In practice this is likely to happen where the conduct of the resident becomes intolerable.) Both cases took the form of an action for damages. In both cases it was held that an agreement for hostel accommodation does not constitute a lease or tenancy, and in so far as it is a contract it can be terminated without prior notice. The decisions are surely correct, but it may be that in the future there will be further attempts of this sort. That the limited funds available to such organisations would be usefully diverted into paying largesse to claimants of this particular type is perhaps not obvious.

The judgment of Sheriff T A K Drummond contains a valuable discussion of the nature of a lease or tenancy.

### (44) Conway v Glasgow City Council 1999 SCLR 248, 1999 Hous LR 20, rev 1999 SLT (Sh Ct) 102, 1999 SCLR 1058, 1999 Hous LR 67

See the previous case.

### (45) Freedman v Edzell Heritable Investment Co 1999 Hous LR 18 (Sh Ct)

A landlord used summary diligence against a tenant, who responded with an action of suspension. The case is a reminder of the dangers of summary diligence: it places great power in the hands of the landlord (or other party).

### (46) Royal Bank of Scotland v Boyle 1999 Hous LR 43 & 63 (Sh Ct)

There was a short assured tenancy under the Housing (Scotland) Act 1988. The lease contained a conventional irritancy for non-payment. **Held**: That it was not enforceable because of disconformity with requirements of the Act.

### (47) West Errol Trust's Trs v Lawrie 1999 SCLR 624 (Sh Ct)

This was a fact-specific case on whether the landlords (of an agricultural holding) had waived their right to enforce a notice to quit.

### (48) Bel Investments Pension Fund Trustees v MacTavish
### 1999 GWD 27–1294 (Sh Ct)

A lease bound the original tenant 'and its successors and assignees all jointly and severally ... to pay ...' the rent. In this action the landlords sued the current tenant plus four previous tenants for unpaid rent. **Held**: that the clause was effective according to its terms. Such clauses are not uncommon. Prospective tenants should be advised in writing as to their existence and effect. They mean that every tenant is, in effect, a cautioner for all future rent. Clients may be surprised, and unhappy, to find themselves asked to pay rent for a property which they ceased to lease many years ago.

### (49) Novacold v Fridge Freight (Fyvie) Ltd
### 1999 SCLR 409 (Sh Ct)

There was a lease of commercial premises. On 25 September 1997 the tenants went into receivership. On 7 October 1997 the landlords obtained warrant to sequestrate for rent. On 8 and 9 October vehicles owned by Volvo Truck and Bus Ltd which were on lease to the tenants were taken back into the possession of the defenders. (How this happened was unclear.) On 10 October 1997 the sequestration was carried out. The vehicles were thus not sequestrated. The landlords sought an order to require the return of the vehicles to the premises. Order granted.

The decision is correct. Leased property is normally subject to the landlord's hypothec (the main exception being agricultural tenancies), and a landlord presumptively has the right to require goods removed from the premises to be returned, so as to protect his interest, albeit nowadays this right is not often exercised. The defenders claimed that the lease of the vehicles had been terminated by the receivership, but in fact the vehicle lease merely provided that the defenders would have an *option* to terminate in the event of receivership, and there was no evidence that that option had in fact been exercised.

### (50) Morrison-Low v Paterson (No 2)
### 1999 GWD 36–1724 (IH)

The landlord sought to terminate an agricultural tenancy. **Held**: that he could not. The facts of the case are unusual, the relationship between the parties being regulated by an earlier decision: *Morrison-Low v Paterson* 1985 SC (HL) 49, 1985 SLT 255.

This affirms the decision of the Lord Ordinary reported at 1998 SLT 564.

### (51) Rose v Bouchet 1999 GWD 20–958 (Sh Ct)

This was an action under the Disability Discrimination Act 1995. The landlord had mentioned that the property might be unsuitable for a blind person because of a missing handrail. The pursuer argued that this constituted illegal discrimination. The action failed, but the case is a reminder of the possible impact of the Act.

## STANDARD SECURITIES AND FLOATING CHARGES

### (52) Bisset v Standard Property Investment plc 1999 GWD 26–1253 (OH)

This is an important case on the duty of a standard security holder to get the best price reasonably obtainable. See **Commentary** p 52.

### (53) Abbey National plc v Arthur 2000 SLT 103 (IH)

A house ('Norden' at Newtonhill, Stonehaven) was owned in common by Douglas Arthur and Charlotte Sutherland. They granted a standard security to the Abbey National. They were both later sequestrated. The Abbey National obtained decree against them granting possession plus warrant for ejection. Thereafter, the Abbey National raised an action to interdict them from entering the property. Interdict was granted, and Sutherland appealed, on the ground that the original action for possession should have been against the trustee in sequestration. The appeal was refused because (1) the first decree had not been reduced and so remained in force, and (2) the first decree was in any case correct. (One might add that any right of challenge which might have existed would presumably have belonged to the trustee in sequestration, anyway, not to Sutherland or Arthur.)

### (54) Société General SA v Lloyds TSB Bank plc 1999 GWD 37–1822 (IH)

The question involved in this case was whether two standard securities secured only a loan of £1,200,000 or whether they also secured other sums due to the standard security holder (Lloyds) as well. The case turned on the proper construction to be put on the documentation, but it is a useful reminder of the importance of clarity in such cases. There has been a good deal of litigation in recent years on this type of issue.

This affirms the decision of the Lord Ordinary reported at 1998 GWD 10–511 and 1999 SLT 649.

### (55) Clydesdale Bank plc v Mowbray 1999 GWD 40–1951 (IH)

This substantially affirms the decision of the Lord Ordinary reported at 1998 GWD 34–1757. It concerns liability for expenses in the enforcement of a standard security.

### (56) Cameron v Abbey National plc 1999 Hous LR 19 (Sh Ct)

What if an assured tenancy is granted by an owner without the consent of an existing standard security holder? If the security is enforced, whose rights prevail? Standard Condition 6 of the Conveyancing and Feudal Reform (Scotland) Act 1970, as interpreted by *Trade Development Bank* v *Warriner & Mason* 1980 SC 74, says that a lease or tenancy granted without the permission of the holder of a pre-existing standard security is voidable at the instance of the secured creditor. Section 18 of the Housing (Scotland) Act 1988 says that 'the Sheriff shall not make an order for possession of a house let on an assured tenancy except on one or more of the grounds set out in Schedule 5'. The second 'ground' in that Schedule is where there is a pre-existing standard security which is being enforced *provided that the tenant had advance notice of its existence*. In practice tenants will seldom receive such notice. Presumably the 1988 Act trumps the 1970 Act, but the subject is obscure. In the present case the tenant obtained an interim interdict against the creditor from evicting him. The case is thus similar to *Tamouri* v *Clydesdale Bank* 1996 SCLR 732. But there seems to be no reported case where the issue has been fully litigated.

### (57) Forsyth v Royal Bank of Scotland plc 2000 SCLR 61 (OH)

Another attempt by a spouse to back out of a standard security on the ground that she signed it by reason of misrepresentation by her husband. See **Commentary** p 55.

[Another aspect of this case is digested at (25).]

### (58) Cowie v Walsh 1999 GWD 15–686 (Sh Ct)

An action for count reckoning and payment. The pursuer alleged that there was an agreement that P and D would co-operate in buying a house, refurbishing and reselling it, and sharing the eventual profit, but that the defender, after having taken title in her name, took possession of the property and repudiated the agreement. D pled that the deal was a *pactum illicitum*, since she had obtained a domestic mortgage and not a commercial one, and so the alleged agreement was unenforceable. **Held**: that this averment did not necessarily mean that the agreement was illegal, and proof before answer allowed.

## NEGLIGENT SURVEYS

### (59) Stewart v Ryden Residential Ltd 1999 GWD 12–576 (OH)

Actions against surveyors are usually in respect of alleged *over*valuation. This action was unusual in that it was a claim for alleged *under*valuation as to the appropriate level of insurance. The flatted property at 69 York Place, Edinburgh, was Grade A listed. The survey report (in 1987) valued the property at £48,000 with the proper level of insurance cover as £110,000. The buyer insured at this value, but after a serious fire it emerged that the property was seriously underinsured for reinstatement purposes. The reason for the error appears to have been that reinstatement costs were calculated on a formula of £101 per square foot but that the surveyors had mismeasured the property and come up with a figure of 1084 square feet instead of the true figure of 1637 square feet. The legal debate was whether the surveyors owed a duty to the buyer, since the survey report was addressed to the seller. (The same solicitors were acting for both sides.) The defenders sought dismissal of the action as irrelevant. Proof before answer was allowed.

# SOLICITORS AND ESTATE AGENTS

### (60) Brady v Neilsons 1999 GWD 4–209 (OH)

John Brady had, over the years, a series of transactions with his brother and sister-in-law, Alistair and Norma Brady, involving loans by him to them and also property transactions between them. Eventually, he was unable to recover a loan. He sued the defenders for not having given him proper advice, in particular in connection with a property at Fernlea, West Lothian, which he had disponed (or rather re-disponed, since they themselves had earlier had the title) to Alistair and Norma, the disposition having been apparently made with the idea that he would be repaid as a result of the development of the property, a development which required title to be vested in Alistair and Norma. The defenders pled that they had acted only for Alistair and Norma and not for the pursuer. Proof was allowed on this question.

The case is of a general type which crops up quite frequently. Without commenting on the facts of this particular case, we would observe that solicitors are not always as aware as they should be of exactly whom they are acting for. There is sometimes a vague idea that they are acting for a certain 'family', without any further precision. This can lead to problems.

### (61) Lomond Assured Properties Ltd v McGrigor Donald
### 1999 GWD 11–512 (OH)

This was an action for damages for negligence. Lomond concluded missives to buy properties at Port Glasgow from Richard Wilson Homes Ltd. For tax reasons it was decided that the price should be paid in advance. It was agreed that the sellers should grant to the buyers standard securities over certain other properties, securing the sellers' obligations under the missives. This was duly carried out. In fact, however, the Bank of Scotland held a first-ranked floating charge. The defenders did not obtain any restriction or ranking agreement from the Bank of Scotland. There was also an alleged failure to obtain NHBC certificates and also a road bond. The sellers went into receivership. The buyers did not have title to the properties they were buying and the construction work was not completed.

Eventually, matters were settled after lengthy negotiations with the receiver but the buyers suffered substantial losses. The defenders admitted negligence but denied that their negligence was the cause of the disaster.

The case is a fact-specific one. It serves, however, as a reminder that when instructions are received to take a standard security from a company it is wise to check whether there is a floating charge in place in favour of another creditor.

### (62)  The Royal Bank of Scotland plc v Harper Macleod
### 1999 GWD 16–733 (Sh Ct)

The pursuers sued for damages, on the basis that they would not have lent (or would have lent less) had they known that there was no title to the top floor, and that the building was a listed one. The case turned on a pleading point. **Held**: that the way that the *esto* plea was framed meant that the pursuers were limited to proof of the lower of the two sums they were claiming.

### (63)  Bristol & West Building Society v Aitken Nairn WS
### 2000 SCLR 47 (IH)

This reverses the decision at first instance reported at 1999 SLT 43. See **Commentary** p 72.

### (64)  Leeds & Holbeck Building Society v Alex Morison & Co
### 1999 GWD 9–434 (OH)

This was also an action by a lender against a law firm. See **Commentary** p 74.

### (65)  G & S Properties Ltd v Henderson 1999 GWD 6–283 (OH)

In recent years there have been numerous cases of estate agents suing for commission. This was yet another example. Mr and Mrs Henderson owned Easterton of Mugdock Farm, near Milngavie. They decided to break it up into lots and market them. The agreed commission was 3%, later reduced to 2%. The main question for decision was whether, on the complex facts of the case, commission was payable. **Held**: that it was.

One aspect of the case deserving mention is that s 18 of the Estate Agents Act 1979 says that if an estate agent uses certain terms these must be explained to the customer. Two of the terms so controlled are 'sole agency' and 'sole selling rights'. The sanction for non-explanation is that the contract is unenforceable except to the extent that the court may, at its discretion, allow. In the present case, the estate agents had breached the Act by using these terms with explanation but it was held that no prejudice had in fact ensued and the breach was accordingly waived.

# BOUNDARY DISPUTES/PRESCRIPTION

### (66) Drummond & Renton v McNeill, Duns Sheriff Court
### 1 September 1999 (unreported)

There were two adjacent properties, numbers 2 and 6 North Street, Duns. Running from the street, and between the properties, was a pend, and at the top of the pend was a yard. The main aspect of the case was a dispute as to which side owned the yard. That was decided in favour of Drummond and Renton, chiefly on the basis of prescriptive possession.

But there was another issue as well. Drummond and Renton also claimed a prescriptive servitude of way over the pend, to the yard, this pend belonging to McNeill. McNeill disputed the existence of such a servitude. Her argument was that prescription in favour of Drummond and Renton could run only when they were owners of the yard. Until they were the owners of the yard there was no dominant tenement in favour of which there could be prescriptive use. Hence, logically there could be no overlap between (a) the 10-year period which conferred on Drummond and Renton prescriptive title to the yard, and (b) the 20-year period needed to constitute a prescriptive servitude of access to the yard along the pend. The 20-year period could start to run only when the 10-year period had been completed. This argument failed, apparently on the ground that the effect of prescription is notionally retrospective.

The issue is one of considerable difficulty, and there are indeed authorities indicating that positive prescription may be considered as operating retrospectively. But we incline to think this to be an incorrect view of the law, and that a person who acquires a prescriptive title does so only from the time when the requisite period has elapsed. Indeed, in property law generally, retrospectivity is excluded. At a given time something either (a) is owned by X, or (b) is not owned by X. For example, if X is owner on a voidable title and the title is reduced, the fact that X was owner (albeit wrongfully) before the reduction is not altered. The past may be regretted but it cannot be changed. Another example is rectification of the Land Register, which is not retrospective: see Case (32) above (*Stevenson-Hamilton's Exrs v McStay*). Likewise, if X is owner of land and Y is in possession and eventually acquires a prescriptive title, the fact that X was owner until the running of prescription had been completed cannot be altered.

# RECTIFICATION OF DOCUMENTS AND REDUCTION

### (67) Bank of Scotland v Brunswick Developments (1987) Ltd (No 2)
### 1999 SC (HL) 53, 1999 SLT 716, 2000 SCLR 30 (HL)

This must surely be the final decision in this long-running saga. A letter of instruction to the Bank of Scotland to transfer £1.5 million was signed by A and by B. A and B were authorised signatories of both company X and company Y.

The letter was written on the stationery of company X and bore to be signed on behalf of company X. In fact (as proof eventually demonstrated) it should have been written on the stationery of company Y and expressed as signed on behalf of company Y. The Bank, which duly transferred the funds, sought rectification of the letter, under s 8(1)(b) of the Law Reform (Miscellaneous Provisions) (Scotland) Act 1985 to the effect of substituting the name of company Y for that of company X.

At procedure roll it was argued that, since s 8(1)(b) applies where a document fails to express accurately the intention of the 'grantor', it cannot therefore be used to alter the actual identity of the grantor. In the end, the First Division got round this difficulty by saying that the true 'grantor' of a deed was the actual signatory (in this case A and B). Hence, a proof was allowed of the alleged error. (See 1995 SLT 689, 1995 SCLR 325.) At the subsequent proof (1997 SLT 48), the Lord Ordinary granted rectification, and this decision was upheld by the First Division (1997 SC 226, 1997 SCLR 500, 1998 SLT 439). The present decision was the appeal to the House of Lords.

In the House of Lords the argument moved away from the rectification point. The question was whether the signatories had been authorised by company Y. They had no actual authority, and the letter could not be taken as indicating to the Bank ostensible authority because it was written on the wrong notepaper. The absence of ostensible authority at the material time could not be cured by the simple device of subsequent rectification. According to Lord Hoffman (at p 718E) 'one might as well rectify the order for the charge of the Light Brigade'. The Bank had made the transfer on the basis of certain documentation, and it was pointless now to change that documentation. This was not an appropriate use of rectification.

On rectification itself, both parties abandoned the position that the 'grantor' of the letter was the signatory. Instead, the grantor was the company itself (company Y), a view accepted by the House of Lords. But the difficulty then was that the company seemed not to have had any intention, as required by s 8(1)(b).

# DILIGENCE AND INSOLVENCY

## (68) Aitken's Tr v Aitken 1999 GWD 39–1898 (OH)

James and Helen Aitken were co-owners of a house at 52 Whitecraig Road, Musselburgh, and also of another property in the same road. James then disponed to Helen, for 'love favour and affection', his half share of the house. Soon afterwards he was sequestrated and the trustee, understandably, sought to reduce this transfer. The defender (Helen) pled that transfer was not truly gratuitous, either (a) because she had orally agreed to convey to him her half share of the other property in return, and/or (b) because she was cautioner for a bank loan of his and in exchange for the disposition of his half share she was prepared to waive her right of relief in the event that she was made to pay. (Argument (b) is not quite in the terms pled, but it seems to be what it boiled down to.) All this was rather flimsy, and the court granted decree of reduction *de plano*.

A lesson for conveyancers is that if they are asked to prepare a gratuitous disposition they should double-check whether it really is gratuitous. (Which in fact it appears to have been in this particular case.) There might be some background consideration which needs to be documented, especially if there is any possibility that the disponer may become bankrupt.

### (69) Souter v Kennedy 23 July 1999, Perth Sheriff Court (unreported)

A case on title to heritable property in a sequestration. See **Commentary** p 62.

## SPECIAL DESTINATIONS

### (70) Fleming's Tr v Fleming 2000 SLT 406 (IH)

An important case on special destinations, overruling *Barclays Bank* v *McGreish* 1983 SLT 344. The case affirms the decision of the sheriff, reported at 1998 SCLR 1070. See **Commentary** p 64.

## MISCELLANEOUS

### (71) B G Hamilton Ltd v Ready Mixed Concrete (Scotland) Ltd 1999 SLT 524 (OH)

The tenant under a 999-year lease registered an *a non domino* conveyance of the landlord's interest. Before prescription could run the landlord challenged the conveyance and argued that it amounted to an implied renunciation of the lease. This argument was rejected by the court. See **Commentary** p 79.

### (72) Pringle's Exr v Pringle 1999 GWD 37–1832 (IH)

Bryan and Heather Pringle were co-owners of 5 Allan Park Loan, Edinburgh. On 26 March 1995 Bryan killed Heather. He was convicted and sentenced for culpable homicide. Although he accepted that he was not entitled to any of Heather's estate he sought to argue that two life assurance policies, in joint names, were not part of her estate because they had been assigned in security of the mortgage loan. This argument was rejected.

### (73) Oliver & Son Ltd Ptnr 16 June 1999 (unreported) (IH)

Travelling people took up occupation of ground at Newmart (otherwise New Mart) Road, Edinburgh. This decision is an important precedent for the procedure to be used in removing such persons when their names are not known to the pursuer.

### (74)  Micro Leisure Ltd v County Properties & Developments Ltd
### 1999 SC 501 (OH)

Section 320 of the Companies Act 1985 provides that a 'non-cash' acquisition or disposal between a company and one of its directors (or a person or company connected with one of its directors) is (subject to exceptions) voidable at the instance of the company unless it has approved the transaction at a general meeting. This case is fact-specific, but it is a useful reminder to conveyancers of a trap into which is all too easy to fall.

# ❧ PART II ❧

PART II

# STATUTORY DEVELOPMENTS

## (A) FINANCE ACT 1999

### Abolition of mortgage tax relief

By s 38 mortgage tax relief is abolished, with effect from 6 April 2000.

### Increased Stamp Duty for conveyances on sale

Section 111 raises the rates of Stamp Duty once again. The new rates are:

| Consideration | Duty | |
|---|---|---|
| 0–60,000 | nil | (unchanged) |
| 60,001–250,000 | 1% | (unchanged) |
| 250,001–500,000 | 2.5% | (up from 2%) |
| 500,000– | 3.5% | (up from 3%) |

These rates apply to all deeds executed on or after 16 March 1999 except where executed in pursuance of a contract made on or before 9 March 1999.

### New method of calculating *ad valorem* Stamp Duty

For deeds executed on or after 1 October 1999, s 112(1) provides that the amount of Stamp Duty payable is to be rounded up to the nearest £5.

### Increase in fixed duties

For Stamp Duty all fixed duties are increased from 50p to £5 (s 112(2)).

### Penalties for late payment

Section 109 inserts a new s 15A and s 15B into the Stamp Act 1891. Stamp Duty is to be paid within 30 days of 'execution' (= delivery) of the deed. If it is paid after this, there is liability both for interest and for a penalty. The maximum penalty which can be imposed is (i) if not later than 1 year, £300, (ii) in any other case, £300 or the amount of duty, whichever is the greater.

## (B) FEES IN REGISTERS OF SCOTLAND (AMENDMENT) ORDER 1999 SI 1999/1085

This increases some fees at the Registers but reduces others. The changes took effect on 21 April 1999.

The cost of reports in the Land Register is increased by around 13.5%. The new fees are as follows (previous fees in brackets):

| | | |
|---|---|---|
| Forms 10, 12, 14, P16 and P17 | £22.70 | (£20) |
| Forms 11 and 13 | £13.60 | (£12) |
| Forms P16/10 and P17/12 | £34 | (£30) |

The cost of inspecting the Registers is, however, reduced, presumably in anticipation of the launch of Registers Direct. So, for example, a Sasine search sheet can now be inspected for £2 (formerly £7), while a search in the Personal Register against six names or fewer is now £3.50 (formerly £7).

## (C) LAND REGISTRATION (SCOTLAND) ACT 1979 (COMMENCEMENT ORDER No 13) SCOTTISH SI 1999/111

This extends the Land Register to the counties of Argyll and Bute, with effect from 1 April 2000. This is in accordance with the revised timetable for extension of the Register published at 1997 SLT (News) 218.

# PART III

# OTHER MATERIAL

## (A) ABOLITION OF THE FEUDAL SYSTEM

In February 1999 the Scottish Law Commission issued its final report (Scot. Law Com. No 168) on the abolition of the feudal system. A bill based on the Law Commission's report is currently before Parliament: see **Commentary** p 74.

## (B) PENALTY CLAUSES

In May 1999 the Scottish Law Commission issued its final report (Scot. Law Com. No 171) on penalty clauses. The report includes a short draft bill, running to six sections. The report recommends a complete re-casting of the law of penalty clauses. A penalty clause is no longer to be judged by reference to whether or not it is a 'pre-estimate' of damages. Instead, the suggested new principle is that a penalty clause should be enforceable except where it is manifestly excessive. And even in such cases it is proposed that the courts should have power to modify the penalty so that it is no longer manifestly excessive. This would apply to all contracts, including those entered into in the course of conveyancing.

## (C) REMEDIES FOR BREACH OF CONTRACT

In December 1999 the Scottish Law Commission issued its final report (Scot. Law Com. No 174) on remedies for breach of contract. Again this applies to missives and other conveyancing contracts. The report includes a short draft bill, running to five sections. These include the displacement of the rule in *White & Carter (Councils) Ltd* v *McGregor* 1962 SC(HL) 1 (*ie* the rule that a party can continue to perform a contract even where the other side has indicated that performance is unwelcome). The proposal is that performance in such circumstances should be subject to a test of reasonability. Another proposal, more important for conveyancers, is that non-patrimonial loss should be recoverable for breach of contract. At present the law is unclear and inconsistent. Examples of non-patrimonial loss would be physical suffering and emotional distress.

## (D) COURT DECISIONS ON THE INTERNET

Decisions of the Scottish courts are now available on the Scottish Courts website. The address is www.scotcourts.gov.uk/ This includes all decisions of the Court of Session, as soon as they are issued, as well as selective decisions of the sheriff court. It is easy to use, and decisions can be searched either by keyword or by subject matter.

## (E) DELAYS IN CONCLUDING MISSIVES

The problem of delay in concluding missives continues, notwithstanding the Guidelines issued in 1998 by the Law Society. For a valuable discussion of the problem see an article by Jenny H Clark, JLSS July 1999, p 15.

## (F) SCOTTISH CONVEYANCING AND EXECUTRY SERVICES BOARD

The Board opened for business on 1 March 1997. Its Annual Report for 1998/99 shows that in its first two years of operation 12 applications were received for registration of which six were successful. Of the successful applicants, only two operate on their own account. The Board estimates that by 1 April 2003 there might be 30 licensed conveyancers and/or executry practitioners, including 12 providing services directly to the public.

## (G) DIRECTORY OF SERVICES FOR CONVEYANCERS

The Law Society has produced a new edition of this valuable guide.

## (H) NEW BOOKS

SIR CRISPIN AGNEW OF LOCHNAW, *Crofting Law* (T&T Clark, 2000)

SIR CRISPIN AGNEW OF LOCHNAW, *Variation and Discharge of Land Obligations* (W. Green, 1999)

NEIL A COLLAR, *Planning* (2nd edn, W. Green, 1999)

D J CUSINE AND R RENNIE, *Missives* (2nd edn, Butterworths, with Law Society of Scotland, 1999)

W M GORDON, *Scottish Land Law* (2nd edn, W. Green, with Scottish Universities Law Institute, 1999)

G L GRETTON AND K G C REID, *Conveyancing* (2nd edn, W. Green, 1999)

DAVID JOHNSTON, *Prescription and Limitation* (W. Green, with Scottish Universities Law Institute, 1999)

ANGUS MCALLISTER AND RAYMOND MCMASTER, *Scottish Planning Law* (2nd edn, Butterworths, 1999)

# PART IV

# COMMENTARY

## MISSIVES

### Risk

In *Homecare Contracts (Scotland) Ltd* v *Scottish Midland Co-operative Society Ltd* 1999 GWD 23–1111 missives contained the following clause:

> With regard to condition 4 of your offer dated 6th January 1995, the risk of damage to or destruction of the subjects shall not pass to the purchaser until the date of entry. In the event that as at the date of entry the subjects shall be materially damaged, then either party shall be entitled, but not bound, to resile from the missives and that by written notice to such effect served upon the other party or its agents not later than the date of entry (time being of the essence). In the event that the purchasers shall elect to proceed to settle the purchase of the subjects the purchasers shall have no claim against the sellers by reason or arising from any such damage or destruction to the subjects but shall be entitled upon demand to receive an assignation of the right to receive any proceeds of insurance effected by the sellers . . .

We mention this case only for two reasons. One is to draw attention to the remarkable timetable imposed by the second sentence. No provision is made for a pre-entry inspection (which, by the way, is a provision worth thinking about for missives in general, and not only where there is a tight timetable). So, strictly, the purchasers could not look over the premises without first settling the transaction. But if they did settle the transaction then, by the third sentence, they could not claim for physical damage. Even if the sellers kindly allowed them to inspect before handing over the money, they would then have to refuse to settle *and*, in the course of the same day, deliver a letter resiling from the bargain. This kind of thing makes it hard to concentrate on the flitting. To labour the obvious, it will be observed that the first sentence is drained of almost all meaning by the second.

The other reason we mention this case is the approach taken by the court. The property was indeed damaged by water penetration. None the less, the purchasers settled (presumably in ignorance) and were now suing for damages. It was difficult to see how this was possible under the clause quoted above. However, the Sheriff Principal allowed a proof on the, perhaps curious, basis that the clause was confined to cases where the subjects were 'materially damaged', and it might be possible to show that the damage was not material. The argument, presumably, is that while no claim can be made for material damage, at least after settlement, non-material damage can be recovered for. Only the lesser harm gives rise to a remedy. Whatever the contract may have said, it is difficult to believe that this is what the parties really intended.

## The reasonable purchaser?

In *Palmer* v *Forsyth* 1999 SLT (Sh Ct) 93 the missives included the following provision:

> The title deeds will be exhibited prior to settlement and will be in terms entirely satisfactory to our clients [ie the purchasers], of which our clients shall be the sole judge, failing which our clients' only option will be to resile from the contract following hereon without penalty.

This is more exacting than the usual clause. The standard set is a subjective one. The terms of the titles need not be objectively bad. All that is required is that the purchasers should think them unsatisfactory. Such clauses place purchasers in a strong position. However, there is at least one situation in which such a clause may work the other way round and prejudice the purchasers. That is where the purchasers decide to go ahead and later find that there is a problem which they had overlooked. Arguably, a clause of the sort quoted would mean that the purchasers would be without remedy, though it could be replied that the right to declare themselves dissatisfied would continue up until the very moment of settlement. Does a clause of this sort wholly oust the implied obligation for good and marketable title? (On that implied obligation, see G L Gretton and K G C Reid, *Conveyancing* (2nd edn, 1999) pp 98–100.) What if there was a problem with the title which did not appear from the 'title deeds' themselves?

In the event, the purchasers *did* think the titles unsatisfactory, and duly resiled. The seller sought damages for breach of contract arguing that (a) the purchasers were not entitled to resile without giving reasons, and (b) that there was an implied term that they would act reasonably, and not capriciously and arbitrarily, in exercising their discretion to resile.

The Sheriff rejected (a), which was not generally supported by the authorities. So a person with a right to resile can do so without giving reasons. Indeed, he might be wise not to give reasons in case his actions are challenged later, and the reasons given turn out not to be the best ones.

The Sheriff accepted (b) but dismissed the action on the basis that it was up to the seller to show in what respects the purchasers' actions were capricious and arbitrary, and there were no averments on this point.

Three comments may be made here. First, the existing case law (reviewed on pp 55–56 of G L Gretton and K G C Reid, *Conveyancing* (2nd edn, 1999)) on implying a reasonableness term is conflicting and unclear. The Sheriff assumed too easily that reasonableness can always be implied.

Second, the decision on (b) does not sit easily with the decision on (a). For if the purchasers were not bound to give reasons for their decision, on what basis could the seller produce detailed averments showing that they had behaved in a manner that was capricious and arbitrary? This approach puts purchasers in a strong position, at least if they take care to hold their tongue. However, there is a suggestion in the judgment that the purchasers might have to give their reasons once the dispute is in court.

Third, and at a practical level, we suggest that conveyancers should think twice before agreeing a clause of the present type. At the least, the clause should be qualified to import a requirement to act reasonably. But this still leaves plenty of scope for dispute as to what is 'reasonable'. If the purchaser is free to proceed or not to proceed as he sees fit, the effect is that of an option agreement. No one would grant an option without consideration, and yet it is surprising how often one sees missives which are so encumbered with conditionalities (of various kinds) that the purchaser is given a virtual free option.

### Supersession: is a claim for damages 'enforcement'?

Section 2 of the Contract (Scotland) Act 1997 displaces the rule in *Winston* v *Patrick* 1981 SLT 41 about supersession of missives. As a result, the delivery of the disposition no longer supersedes the missives. But since missives would then (in the main) last for the full 20 years of long negative prescription, it may be a good idea to limit their duration by appropriate provision in the missives. If that view is taken, then in place of the traditional *non*-supersession clause what is now required is a supersession clause—that is, a clause which expressly provides that missives should come to an end after a certain period of time. A typical supersession clause would be the following:

> The missives of sale of which this offer forms part shall cease to be enforceable after a period of two years from the date of entry hereunder except insofar as they are founded on in any court proceedings which have commenced within that period.

The effect of such a clause—or so one might think—is that after two years the missives are dead. But that view was challenged by the decision of Lord Philip in *Smith* v *Lindsay & Kirk* 1998 SLT 1096, 1998 SCLR 572. That decision has since been appealed, and the judgment of the First Division, issued on 16 December 1999, is reported at 2000 SLT 287.

The facts were these. The pursuers concluded missives to buy land. The land included a steading building. In terms of the missives the seller was to convert the building into a dwellinghouse. The transaction duly settled. Both missives and disposition contained a two-year non-supersession clause. (This sale was prior to the Contract (Scotland) Act 1997.) When the seller defaulted on his obligation, the defenders (who were the pursuers' solicitors) failed to raise an action for damages within the two-year period. So the pursuers sued the defenders.

At first instance, the action was dismissed. According to Lord Philip, a contract is 'enforced' where an action is raised for its implement. It is not 'enforced' in an action for damages. He accepted the argument for the defenders that 'an action for damages is not a means of enforcing a contract, but a means of seeking compensation for failure to perform' (p 1098F). Accordingly, the two-year clause did not prevent an action *for damages* being raised outwith the two-year period.

The implications of this decision for the new supersession clause were plain. A clause which put a two-year time limit on enforceability would not prevent a claim for damages being made outwith the two-year period.

This rather surprising decision has now been reversed by the First Division. While the court accepted that 'enforce' is sometimes used in the sense of specific implement, it was plain that the word could also have a wider meaning, and equally plain that that wider meaning was the one intended in the clause under consideration. In that context, 'enforce' must be regarded as including any claim made under the contract, including a claim for damages.

What are the implications for the drafting of supersession clauses? In the light of Lord Philip's decision, we suggest, in the second edition of our book on *Conveyancing*, that 'enforceable' should be replaced by 'founded upon'. A complete clause might then look like this:

> The missives of sale of which this offer forms part may not be founded upon after a period of two years from the date of entry hereunder except in court proceedings commenced within that period.

One of the judges in the First Division went out of his way to endorse this suggestion. According to Lord Milligan:

> I . . . agree with the comment in *Conveyancing* (Professors Gretton and Reid, 2nd edition (1999) footnote 13 on page 281 . . .) . . . that, while the word 'enforceable' has been standard, 'founded upon' may be better . . . in the absence of any suggested disadvantage of such clarifying change.

However, the effect of the decision of the First Division is to leave the choice open on this point. Probably there is little to choose between the two versions. Our inclination, however, is to prefer the 'enforceable' of the original version, for two reasons. First, following the decision of the First Division we now know, as a positive fact, that 'enforceable' does the trick. It is not, after all, too narrow. And second, there might possibly be a danger that 'founded upon' might turn out to be too wide. It might mean more than seeking a remedy under the contract. For example, suppose that, two years after settlement, the granter of a disposition wants to have the deed judicially rectified on the ground that it is disconform to missives. This is not a question of 'enforcing' the missives. But is it 'founding on' them? The answer seems in doubt.

Before leaving this subject, we would point out that a two-year supersession clause is not necessarily the right approach in all cases. Experience shows that it is sometimes not long enough. And there is scope for arguing that it should be dropped altogether. But at all events *non*-supersession clauses should no longer be used. We mention this because, more than two years after the Contract (Scotland) Act 1997, some law firms are still using them in their standard styles.

# LEASES

## Who takes the rents?

Suppose that a creditor has a standard security over commercial property which is subject to a lease. The owner/debtor/landlord becomes insolvent. The creditor can, of course, sell the property, and a buyer will be found who is interested in the investment. But what about the rental stream in the meantime? Who takes that? Can the standard security holder claim it? If the property can be realised at a value above the amount of the debt, the issue will not usually become important. But if there is any prospect of a shortfall upon realisation, the question of entitlement to the rental stream for the period prior to the sale of the property may be a very important one.

In principle, it is and always has been the law that the heritable creditor can claim that rental stream. But the details can give rise to problems. In *UCB Bank plc* v *Hire Foulis Ltd* 1999 SC 250, 1999 SLT 950, 1999 SCLR 35 (IH) the pursuers, a bank, held a standard security over commercial property, which was let out. The owner/debtor/landlord went into insolvent liquidation late in 1996. The bank served a calling-up notice on 4 February 1997, and by agreement with the liquidator they became entitled to the rental stream as from 10 February 1997. The bank then asked the liquidator to pay over to them the rent which had been collected by the liquidator in the period between the start of the liquidation and 10 February. The liquidator refused and the bank sued.

The bank was assisted by an opinion of the late Professor Halliday, saying that in this situation the liquidator is bound to account to the heritable creditor for the rents which he has collected. (See D J Cusine (ed) *Conveyancing Opinions of Professor J M Halliday* (1992) p 32.) And a basis for that view can certainly be found in the 1970 Act. Standard Condition 10 provides that 'when the debtor is in default, the creditor . . . may enter into possession of the security subjects and may receive or recover . . . the rents . . .' The debtor had been in 'default' since the commencement of the liquidation, because the very fact of going into liquidation itself amounts to 'default.' (See Standard Condition 9(1)(c).) Hence from the onset of the liquidation the heritable creditor was entitled to 'receive or recover . . . the rents'.

At first instance, the court accepted that view of matters. The liquidator appealed to the Inner House and was successful. The view taken by the Inner House was that a heritable creditor does not have a right to demand the rents merely by his status as such. He can no more insist that the liquidator should account to him for rents duly received than he could insist that the company itself should have done so, prior to liquidation. Until the creditor takes the appropriate steps towards enforcement, he has no right to the rents. On this view, Standard Condition 10, quoted above, means only that as from the onset of the liquidation the heritable creditor was *entitled* to take possession. ('Possession' in this context means civil possession—*ie* indirect possession—only, since obviously natural possession is held by the lessee.)

## Leases to partnerships

Suppose there is a lease to a partnership. Perhaps it is a farming partnership and the property is agricultural land. Or, perhaps, it is a legal partnership and the property is a town-centre office. And suppose that the partnership is dissolved. Does that bring the lease to an end? Or suppose that the partnership is not dissolved but that there are changes in its membership, by retiral or assumption or death. Might that terminate the lease?

That such questions can seriously be asked is, or should be, surprising. Leases to partnerships have been common for at least 200 years, and one might expect the law in this area to be pretty well clear and settled. The truth is that it is not.

In cases of this sort it is sometimes the tenant who wishes to argue that the lease is at an end. That is likely to be so if the lease is a longish one and the rental level is high. Everyone knows of cases of 25-year commercial leases without break options and with upward-only review clauses, where market rental levels in the area have in fact fallen, where the tenants would be only too happy to be able to bail out. In other cases—and these are perhaps more numerous—it will be the landlord who is keen to see a lease at an end. This is sometimes so in agricultural leases. In yet other cases, the landlord and the tenant may be closely associated and have an identity of economic interest, and the question whether or not a lease terminates may be of significance in a tax context. Indeed, all three sorts of cases have been before the courts—the cases where the tenant wants out, cases where the landlord wants the tenant out, and the tax cases.

We said that the issue may arise (a) on the dissolution of the firm or (b) on a change of membership. One of the problems of the Scots law of partnership is that whilst it is well-settled that a partnership is a separate juristic *persona*, it is not clear whether every change in membership technically creates a new *persona*. In a case in 1927 it was said that:

> There is of course no doubt that every change in the constitution of a firm, whether by the death or retiral of an existing partner, or by the introduction of a new partner, involves a change of the *persona* with important results on existing contracts.
>
> (Lord Constable in *Garden Haig Scott & Wallace* v *Prudential Approved Society for Women* 1927 SC 393.)

Does the law indeed go as far as that? Is it the case that the great law firms, which stretch back over the generations, may not have a single ongoing identity but instead may be really a crowd of economically connected but none the less legally distinct juristic persons? If such a firm deposits £1,000 in a bank for a year, is it really true that the firm at the end of the year might not be the same person as the firm which deposited the money? The answer is probably affirmative—that is to say that Lord Constable was probably right—though there is scope for argument.

A dissolution of this sort—*ie* where the there is a change in membership but the firm continues in being as an economic unit—is sometimes called a 'technical dissolution'.

But if that is the law, does it make any difference if the partnership deed expressly provides that the partnership shall *not* be dissolved by changes in its membership? We would incline to the view that in such a case the *persona* continues as one and the same *persona*. That view is supported by s 33 of the Partnership Act 1890 which says that a partnership is dissolved by the death or bankruptcy of any member, but adds that this is subject to agreement to the contrary. (By the way, s 33 does *not* say that the assumption of a new partner triggers dissolution.) One of the problems about s 33 is that it does not distinguish between (a) dissolution of the contract of partnership, and (b) dissolution of the juristic personality. In theory, at least, the contract might be dissolved but the *persona* continue, and, conversely, the *persona* might be dissolved but the contract continue. The whole subject is deeply obscure, and this is not the place to resolve all the difficulties.

There are at least three possible situations;

- a true dissolution;
- a technical dissolution, where there is a change of membership in an ongoing firm, but the partnership agreement says nothing about deemed continuity;
- the situation where there is a change of membership and the partnership deed expressly provides that such changes shall not change the identity of the firm.

But to what extent these three situations may have different legal consequences is uncertain.

The position is yet further complicated by the fact that the authorities identify a doctrine known as that of 'contracts with a house'. A 'house' is a firm which, despite 'technical dissolutions' continues in being as an economic entity. In terms of this doctrine it is possible, in certain cases, for a contract with a partnership to be created whereby the contract automatically transmits to the successor firm, both as to rights and as to liabilities. However, this doctrine of a 'contract with a house', though it certainly exists, has never been properly developed, either by the courts or by academic writers, and attempts to plead it in the courts have pretty well uniformly been unsuccessful. What one usually sees is the judges saying that the doctrine does exist but that on the facts of the case before them it happens to be inapplicable.

Another dimension to the problem is the form which the lease itself takes. Indeed, this is the key factor. Sometimes, a lease is granted to the firm itself. Sometimes it is granted to the partners, or some of them, as trustees for the firm. Very often a hybrid form is seen, in which (most strangely) the lease is granted to the firm *and* to the partners of the firm as trustees of the firm. A further relevant factor is that the lease may expressly or implicitly allow assignation, or expressly or implicitly forbid it, or allow it conditionally, and this is a vitally important factor in establishing the effect on a lease of dissolution of the firm.

In 1999 another important decision was made on this whole subject, *Moray Estates Development Co v Butler* 1999 SLT 1338, 1999 SCLR 447 (OH). Here there was an agricultural lease granted in 1964 in these terms:

> It is contracted . . . between the parties following viz:—Moray Estates Development Company . . . on the one part and Grigor Butler residing at East Grange, Kinloss by

Forres, Mrs Dorothea Douglas Ritchie Butler, wife of and residing with the said Grigor Butler, and Anthony Butler, residing at Ordies, Alves aforesaid, the partners of the firm of Messrs Grigor Butler & Son, Farmers, Ordies Farm, by Forres, on the other part in manner following:—The said Moray Estates Development Company . . . hereby let to the said Grigor Butler, Mrs Dorothea Douglas Ritchie Butler and Anthony Butler, the partners of the said firm of Messrs Grigor Butler & Son as trustees for the said firm and the survivors and survivor of them as trustees and trustee foresaid . . . excluding heirs and assignees legal or voluntary possessors for behoof of creditors, sub-tenants, and legatees under the Agricultural Holdings (Scotland) Acts, all and whole the farm of Ordies in the Parish of Alves and County of Moray . . .

At that time the partnership deed apparently had no clause providing for the continuity of the firm in the event of changes in membership. Such a clause was added in 1980. Dorothea died in 1988 and later there were other changes in the membership of the partnership. The landlords seem to have become aware of these changes late in 1997 or early in 1998. They saw their opportunity. They raised an action of declarator that 'the Farm of Ordies, by Forres, Moray, is unencumbered by any tenancy in favour of the defenders or any of them or any partnership of which they or any of them may be a partner'. (This was rather neat drafting, for it avoided the problem of specifying precisely when the lease had terminated.) This action succeeded. Although the conclusion of the summons did not seek to put a date on the termination of the lease, the Lord Ordinary opined that the lease had ended *ipso facto* on the first change of membership, namely the death of Dorothea in 1988.

*Moray Estates* will now join the other modern leading cases in this area, namely *Inland Revenue* v *Graham's Trs* 1971 SC (HL) 1, *Jardine-Paterson* v *Fraser* 1974 SLT 93 and *Lujo Properties Ltd* v *Green* 1997 SLT 225. If a coherent doctrine can be developed in this area, it will have to be based mainly on these cases. It is interesting that in three of these four cases it was held that change of membership did automatically terminate the lease, the exception being *Lujo*.

Whether such a coherent doctrine can be developed is uncertain. This whole area is messy. We would suggest the following propositions by way of a hypothesis, but we would stress that it is only a hypothesis.

(1) The effect of dissolution—whether a 'real dissolution' or a 'technical' dissolution—falls to be judged primarily by the terms of the lease itself. That is the controlling document.

(2) If the lease is not assignable, the dissolution of the firm (whether 'real' or 'technical') will terminate the lease *ipso facto*. (See *Graham's Trs* and *Jardine-Paterson*. And *cf MacFarlane* v *Falfield Investments Ltd* 1998 SLT 145.) But this is subject to (1) above.

(3) The fact (if it is a fact) that the partnership agreement provides for continuity notwithstanding changes in membership is probably in itself irrelevant to the construction of the lease. But if the partnership deed itself already contained, before the lease, a provision that it would not be dissolved by change in membership, then it *may* be that the lease will not terminate. That at least seems to be the implication of *Quarantelli* v *Forbes* 2000 GWD

2–67, but *Moray Estates* can be read in an opposite sense. One way of reading *Moray Estates* is that there can be *delectus personae* not merely as to the *tenant*, but, where the tenant is a firm, as to the *membership* of the tenant, with the result that (if there is this special sort of *delectus personae*) a change in membership will terminate the lease, even if it can be shown that there has been no dissolution of the firm.

(4) If a lease is to a group of persons who are in fact partners, but the lease itself does not identify them as partners or mention the partnership, then the dissolution of the firm (whether 'real' or 'technical') probably has no effect on the lease (*cf Morrison-Low* v *Paterson* 1985 SC (HL) 49, 1985 SLT 255, though that was not the point litigated. The original lease in that case seems to have been to three persons in partnership, but the lease seems to have been to them ostensibly as individuals.)

(5) If a lease is to a firm as such and is freely assignable, the dissolution of the firm does not terminate the lease. The partners can assign the lease and will have to do so if they wish to escape the burden of the rent. The same applies in the case where the lease is assignable if the landlord grants consent, such consent not to be withheld unreasonably. This is subject to (1) above.

(6) It seems to make no difference if the lease, instead of being to the firm as such, is to named persons 'as partners' or 'as trustees' for the firm. That, at least, is what the cases indicate, but the correctness of that approach must surely be open to debate.

(7) If, after a dissolution, the firm (or 'successor' firm) continues in possession and continues to pay the rent, and the landlord allows the possession to continue and accepts the rent, it may be the case that a new lease is constituted *rebus ipsis et factis*, and the fact that either side was proceeding in error is irrelevant.

This last proposition is speculative. (They all are, for that matter.) It is based on *Morrison-Low* v *Paterson* 1985 SC (HL) 49. This was a lease to A and B and C who were, it seems, actually partners, but the lease bore to be to them as individuals. On the death of the last of them on 4 December 1974 it was common ground that the lease ended but none the less it continued *de facto*. Lord Keith said:

The true position in law was that the 1929 lease gave the defenders, at all events after 4 December 1974, no right or title to possession of the farm. The landlord did not know this. But the fact remains that he did maintain the defenders in possession of the farm, he did demand and accept rent from them, and he did allow them to carry out improvements. It does not avail him to say that he would not have done so had he known the true legal position. The defenders' possession was not capable of being ascribed in law to the 1929 lease. It must, therefore, be ascribed to something else, and that something else can only be an agreement. The parties did in fact agree, as demonstrated by the possession of the defenders and the acceptance of rent by the landlord. The circumstance that both had been misled about the legal position is irrelevant. The former legal basis for the defenders' possession came to end on 4 December 1974, and, as later events demonstrate, the new one came into existence at the same time.

Admittedly that was not strictly speaking a partnership case, but it is difficult to see why the ratio should not apply to cases of partnership.

In *Morrison-Low* it seems that the landlord was in possession of all the facts, but that both sides were mistaken as to the rights accruing from those facts. The irrelevance of error of which Lord Keith speaks may thus be only the irrelevance of error of *law*, not of error of *fact*. In *Moray Estates*, by contrast, it seems that the landlords did not become aware of the facts until a late stage and that once they became aware they quickly took steps to have the lease declared at an end. (On the other hand, is not death said to be a *public* fact?) Hence the doctrine enunciated by Lord Keith may have had no application to the circumstances which arose in *Moray Estates*. Presumably that was the view taken by counsel, for *Morrison-Low* seems not to have been cited.

But one can imagine some rather strange situations arising out of cases of the *Moray Estates* type. It might easily be that a great many years might pass before the landlords learned of the facts which terminated the lease. During that time both sides believed there to be a valid lease and over the years possession was retained, rent paid and so on. The implication of *Moray Estates* seems to be that the possession will have been, over all those years, unlawful, and, likewise, the rent will not have been a true rent, for there can be a rent only where there is a lease or tenancy. Is the result that all the rent is repayable, with the landlord having a corresponding right to claim money to compensate him for the years of unlawful possession of his land? The implications are disturbing. It is tempting to say, in the interests of common sense and practicality, that Lord Keith's approach in *Morrison-Low* ought to be given a broad generous field of application.

From the standpoint of the conveyancer, the lesson is that leases to partnerships need to be approached with the utmost care, and that styles are even less reliable here than they generally are. The first step is to find out from the clients what they actually want. Lack of clarity about that is the first chapter of all sorts of disasters, and not just in this particular area of law. Once the intentions have been established, the lease can be drafted. Never mind the technical terms: set out in words of one syllable what the agreement is.

# SERVITUDES

## Servitude of necessity

*Inverness Seafield Development Co Ltd* v *Mackintosh* 1999 GWD 31–1497 concerns the interaction of two key rules of conveyancing. The first is the rule that, unless the contract provides otherwise, a disposition can only be drawn in standard terms. More particularly, a disposition cannot impose real burdens or servitudes unless these are already provided for in the missives.

The second is the rule that, in certain circumstances, a servitude will be implied into a disposition. For example—to take the easiest case (as well as the one which actually arose in *Inverness Seafield Development*)—if land is divided and a plot sold, and one of the plots turns out to be landlocked, it is settled law that, in the absence of contrary evidence, there is to be implied into the conveyance a servitude of way for the benefit of the landlocked plot. This is so even if that is the plot being retained—despite the rule that in general a person is taken not to derogate from his own grant.

The facts of the case were that the pursuers had an option, in terms of missives, to buy two further plots of land, or parts thereof. They elected to buy a part plot. Since the effect would have been to leave the remainder of the plot landlocked, the disposition offered by the defenders included an express servitude in their favour over the land being sold. This was resisted.

The novelty of the facts was that the proposed servitude was to be an express one. The argument, in other words, was not that the servitude was to be implied into the *disposition* (though no doubt if it was silent on the subject, that would be the result in law). Rather the argument was that the servitude was to be implied into the earlier *contract* so that the pursuers were entitled to an express servitude in the disposition. This argument was accepted by Lord Johnson. The defenders were held to be entitled to include an express servitude in the disposition.

The convenience of this approach is obvious. It is far better to get things sorted at the time when the disposition is granted, rather than to argue later about whether a deed which was silent on the subject could none the less be regarded as importing a servitude. As a practical matter, the Keeper will not normally enter a servitude on the Land Register unless it is stipulated for in a deed: see 1997 JLSS 507. The approach also means that essential servitudes do not have to be stipulated for in the missives (though, naturally, it is prudent to do so).

Another question was the terms on which the servitude should be granted. Unsurprisingly, the servitude drafted by the defenders was quite wide, including vehicular as well as pedestrian access. Lord Johnston, however, regarded this as acceptable:

> Counsel is quite correct, in my opinion, to submit that this is a wide right permitting further uses than mere agricultural use but that seems to me to be the normal right that would attach to any access to any particular piece of land whether granted impliedly or expressly. Restrictions may be imposed expressly but if one is looking purely at the generality of an implied right of general access, I consider the law does not permit that any specific restrictions should be imposed save if necessary with regard to the basic implication. That is not the case here.

No issue arose as to the *route* of the access because there was an existing track.

## Dangerous servitudes

A servitude must be exercised *civiliter*, that is to say reasonably and in the manner least burdensome to the servient tenement. But what if its exercise is actually dangerous whether to the servient proprietor, or indeed to the dominant proprietor? This may still be the least burdensome manner of exercise, but the burden may seem unacceptable.

Fortunately, most servitudes are not dangerous. But in *Cloy v T M Adams & Sons* 1999 GWD 19–908 the danger was all too apparent. Here, there was a servitude of way over the top of a dam wall belonging to the servient proprietor. The dam was in a parlous condition, and it seemed that if the dominant proprietor, a farmer, continued to drive over it, there was a material danger that the dam would be breached. This would threaten the house belonging to the servient proprietors, as well as causing risk to the life and limb of the dominant proprietor.

Interdict was granted. A servitude which could not be exercised *civiliter* could not be exercised at all. It was pointed out that even if the farmer had actually owned the dam, the law of nuisance would not allow him to use it if such use threatened the pursuers' house. But here his rights were less than those of ownership.

There was a possible argument that the poor state of the dam was due to work carried out by the pursuers. But in that case the remedy of the farmer was said not to be to carry on using the servitude but to sue for damages.

## Interpretation

*Axis West Ltd* v *Chartwell Land Investments Ltd* 1999 SLT 1416 is unusual in that it was a servitude case which went all the way to the House of Lords. If only for that reason, the case deserves mention here.

The litigation arose out of a development site just off Great Western Road in Glasgow. Originally, the site was owned by Atlas Investments. Atlas then sold a part of the site to Chartwell Land Investments Ltd. Clause 2.1.1 of a deed of conditions executed by both parties granted to Chartwell the following servitude:

> for the purposes of carrying out and completing the Chartwell Development and the Common Car Park to make use of and to make connections to all or any electricity cables, telephone wires and/or cables, gas and water supply pipes, drains and sewers and other like services currently serving the Atlas Subjects or any part or parts thereof.

The 'Atlas Subjects' were being retained by Atlas. The development site also included other property still owned by Atlas, including a distributor road. Subsequently, Atlas sold the road to Axis West Developments Ltd.

The main surface water drain, already in place at the time of the deed of conditions, was under the distributor road. This drain served the Atlas subjects. Accordingly, Chartwell ran a pipe which connected directly into this drain. Their right to do so was challenged by Axis, the owner of the road. Ultimately, the dispute seems to have been about money. Axis wanted to be paid the market rate for the servitude which, in their view, Chartwell needed in order to lay the pipe under the road.

The dispute focused on the final words of clause 2.1.1. Axis' argument was that servitudes fall to be interpreted strictly. On a strict interpretation, the clause conferred no more than a right to lay pipes under the Atlas subjects. There was no right to lay pipes under the distributor road. Chartwell founded on the express terms of the clause. This conferred a right to make connections to drains, etc 'currently serving the Atlas subjects'. The only question to be determined was whether, as at the date of the deed of conditions, the drain under the distributor road served the Atlas subjects. If it did, Chartwell had a right to connect into it. It did not matter that the drain did not itself lie in the Atlas subjects.

The First Division had found for Chartwell, and the House of Lords agreed. On close scrutiny, the words of the clause bore out the interpretation argued for by Chartwell.

A number of more general points come out of the decision. First, Lord Hope said this about the identification of the servient tenement (p 1418 K–L):

> The deed which grants the servitude does not need to define the extent of the servient tenement, because the servient tenement is taken to be the whole land over which it was granted which was in the ownership of the grantor at the date of the deed . . . [I]f the grantor wishes to limit the extent of his land which is subject to the servitude, he may do so by including a provision to this effect in the deed.

The presumption, therefore, is that all of the grantor's land is affected. In the present case, Atlas owned the distributor road as well as the so-called Atlas Subjects. Thus, in the absence of qualifying words, both were subject to the servitude.

Second, the argument for Chartwell depended on the admissibility of extrinsic evidence, for it was necessary to show which drains, etc served the Atlas Subjects at the time of the deed of conditions. But was such extrinsic evidence competent? And if not, were the words of the clause sufficiently precise to create a servitude? Here Lord Hope took an appropriately relaxed view (p 1419 H):

> I think that it is clear that the degree of precision which is required will vary according to the subject matter and what is practicable. The facts that the location and extent of each of the various services mentioned in the clause will have to be determined by reference to extrinsic evidence such as maps or plans does not deprive the clause of the necessary degree of certainty. It was not suggested that the description which was used in this case has given rise in practice to any difficulty.

Conveyancers will be heartened by the reference to 'what is practicable'. No doubt, of course, it would have been possible to prepare a plan at the time of the deed of conditions showing the location of the services. But Lord Hope suggests that what is possible is not necessarily practicable or sensible. The law will make do with less.

Finally, Lord Clyde's judgment makes some use of a case from South Africa. This is a sign of the times. The political changes in that country have made it acceptable once again to look at its law. And it turns out—as indeed the late T B Smith used to tell us—that South African law is often remarkably close to Scots law, particularly in the field of property law. The particular case discussed in *Axis West Developments* was sourced through the excellent new book on *Servitudes and Rights of Way*, by Douglas Cusine and Roddy Paisley, which cites a number of South African authorities. South African authorities are also being cited to the Scottish courts in other areas. Practitioners need to be alerted to this new development. (South African legal materials can be found, among other places, in Edinburgh University Law Library. Current decisions of the supreme courts are now available electronically at http://www.law.wits.ac.za/sca/scadate.html). Indeed, there are signs that the Scottish courts are more interested than they used to be in comparative law of all sorts. In the next section it will be seen how

Australian authority is shaping the law of standard securities. But South African law is in a category of its own in terms of relevance.

# STANDARD SECURITIES

### Duty to get the best price reasonably obtainable

When a standard security holder enforces and sells, he is under an obligation to get the best price reasonably obtainable. That is an obligation under the common law, and it is also expressly laid down in s 25 of the Conveyancing and Feudal Reform (Scotland) Act 1970. Breach of it will expose the heritable creditor to an action for damages. The rule is an important one, for an obvious reason. Suppose that there is a secured loan of £60,000 and the property is worth £100,000. The lender, on enforcing the security, has no incentive to obtain a price higher than £60,000 plus expenses, for he will not gain by any excess over that amount. Therefore, the law must impose such an incentive.

In the case of ordinary residential property the duty is usually fairly easy to discharge. Such properties have a pretty definite market value and there is a pretty standard way of marketing them. It is hard for a heritable creditor to go badly wrong. (Having said that, one does hear some horror stories of properties which are sold without any real attempt at advertisement.)

The duty becomes more difficult for many other kinds of property, and especially property with possible development value, and also property which might appeal to buyers furth of Scotland. Where should it be advertised? Should developers be approached? Should outline planning permission be sought? Should the property be offered in lots? Whereas a house in a town usually has a fairly well-defined market value, *ie* a narrowish band of value about which there is very limited scope for argument, for other properties the band can be much wider, especially if there is some possibility for development. Reasonable opinions as to value may vary considerably, and an objective valuation in retrospect is extremely difficult because it is difficult to disregard the benefit of hindsight. For instance, if planning permission is granted in 2001 it is difficult to keep knowledge of that fact out of mind when estimating the value as at 1999.

A heritable creditor can all too easily get it wrong, and then be accused of having failed to discharge his common law and statutory duties.

In *Bisset* v *Standard Property Investment plc* 1999 GWD 26–1253 (OH) there was a standard security over the Bridge of Orchy Hotel, by Glencoe. After default on the loan the creditors offered the hotel for sale by roup (December 1993). There were no bids. At a second roup in February 1996 the hotel was sold at its reserve price to a company connected with the creditors. The former owners sued the creditors for damages for failure to sell for the best price reasonably obtainable. They had a catalogue of complaints about the way the sale was handled, including that sale by roup was inappropriate, that the development potential was not explored, that the property was not properly advertised, and so on.

The case has a number of interesting features, but the most important is that the defenders pled that the whole action was irrelevant, because *esto* there had been faults (which, of course, they denied), they had entrusted the marketing to a reputable firm of estate agents, and that was a sufficient discharge of their obligations.

This position was rather a strong one. In *Dick* v *Clydesdale Bank* 1991 SLT 678 Lord President Hope said that 'in the ordinary case the creditor may be regarded as having fulfilled the duties imposed upon him in regard to the marketing of the subjects if he takes and acts upon appropriate professional advice.'

This was the position that the pursuers had to challenge, and they did so successfully. The Lord Ordinary (Hamilton) observed that Lord Hope's remark was *obiter*. The court was much influenced by an Australian case (which had not been cited to the court in *Dick*), namely *Commercial and General Acceptance Ltd* v *Nixon* [1983] 152 CLR 491. In that case, the question of whether relying on professional advice is a sufficient defence was examined closely, and the High Court affirmed the decision of the Queensland Supreme Court that it is not a sufficient defence. A mortgagee does not, indeed, have an absolute, or strict, liability. But it is not enough merely to abandon the whole matter to agents. The High Court took the view that a mortgagee must take the same care as an owner would if he asked agents to market the property for him. An owner would not normally sit back and do nothing. He would keep an eye on the agents to make sure that they were doing their job. A mortgagee selling must, therefore, do the same. Given that s 85 of the Queensland Property Law Act was in substantially similar terms to s 25 of our own Act, Lord Hamilton was prepared to adopt the position of the High Court, and thus effectively not to follow Lord Hope's *dictum* in *Dick*. The result was that the pursuers had a case which was entitled to go to proof.

We do not know whether the decision will be reclaimed. We incline to agree with Lord Hamilton. There is a balance to be struck. It would be unfair to impose too high a standard on selling creditors. They cannot know as much about (for instance) development potential or potential buyers as the owners. Moreover, ex-owners usually have inflated ideas about the value of their former property and the law should not encourage vexatious actions. But on the other hand it is, we feel, not acceptable for a selling creditor to disclaim all responsibility for a sale at (alleged) undervalue by hiding behind the fact that he instructed agents.

That was the main issue in the case but there were some other important points as well. One was the question of whether a selling creditor has an absolute discretion as to whether to sell by private bargain or by roup. (As a matter of history such sales originally had to be by roup (as is still the case in many countries), and the possibility of sale by private bargain is relatively modern.) Lord Hamilton took the view that whilst there is a discretion it is not an absolute one and that it is open to a disgruntled ex-owner to argue that in the particular case roup was inappropriate.

Another point was whether a creditor has complete discretion as to the timing of the sale. Once again in *Dick* there were *dicta* so asserting. Once again Lord

Hamilton expressed doubt about the correctness of that view, though it does not seem that he had to make a decision on the point.

Yet another point of interest concerned the burden of proof. Normally in an action of this sort it is for the pursuer to prove that the defender has been in breach. But in this case the purchasers had been a company connected with the heritable creditors, and it was a matter of concession that in such circumstances the burden of proof was reversed, and it was for the heritable creditors to show that they were not in breach. The concession was well founded, in the light of *Davidson* v *Scott* 1915 SC 924. There, a sale was made to a company in which the heritable creditor had a controlling interest, and it was held that the burden of proof was reversed.

The issue is far from being an esoteric one. Some institutional lenders do sell to a connected company when they have difficulties in achieving a decent price in the ordinary way. This practice can have certain commercial advantages. For if the property is dumped on the market at a knock-down price, the lender suffers an immediate loss. (In theory, the debtor is liable for the balance of the loan but in practice this is often irrecoverable.) But if the property is sold at a decent figure to a connected company, no loss is taken in the group accounts at this stage. If, later on, the property proves difficult to shift, it can be dumped at that stage and the loss taken then. If that happens, the lender is no worse off. But it may be that after a year or two or three the property can be sold at a decent price, in which case the lender (or, rather, the group of which the lender forms a part) has saved itself a great deal of money. If all this is done in an appropriate way, it is perfectly proper and, far from prejudicing the debtor, can actually benefit him by achieving a sale price higher than would otherwise have been achieved. But it is evidently not without risk, in that challenge is easier.

Another complaint of the pursuers was that the creditors had not realised an insurance policy over which they held a security. Had the creditors done so, the capital sum due would have been reduced and, with it, the interest burden. Lord Hamilton had no difficulty in rejecting that complaint.

Finally, we would observe that in cases of this sort the real issue, at the end of the day, is the factual one of whether a fair price has actually been achieved. If it has been achieved then any irregularity in the marketing of the property will be merely *injuria sine damno*—a wrong which has, in the event, caused no loss. Likewise, if it can be shown that a fair price has not been achieved then there is prima facie liability without the need to prove irregularity in the marketing.

## The 'surety wife'—again

One of the issues of the day concerns the 'surety wife'. (Of course, it does not have to be a woman, and it does not have to be a spouse. But in reality it is usually the wife. So we don't apologise for the political incorrectness. Perhaps we should apologise for using the English term 'surety' but it is convenient in this context.)

The husband is in business. His business needs to borrow from the bank. The bank wants security for the loan. The husband suggests that the family home be used. But it is co-owned, and so the wife will have to sign too. So she signs a standard security. Her husband's business fails and he becomes insolvent. The bank calls up the standard security and she is faced with losing her home. She seeks to repudiate the security. She claims that her husband induced her to sign by misrepresentations or even by threats. If the marriage is intact—and sometimes even if it is not—the husband is likely to corroborate her story, for this is likely to be the only chance to save any assets from the wreck. The difficulty which lies in the wife's way is that even if there were such misrepresentations or threats, they were the husband's fault, not the bank's, so why should the bank suffer? That was, indeed, the position taken by Scots law until the land-mark case of *Smith* v *Bank of Scotland* 1997 SC (HL) 111. In that case it was held ... well, what was held? No one is quite sure. (For Professor Gretton's attempts to state a ratio for the case see 1997 SLT (News) 195.) Probably it held that if the bank knows that the parties are in some sort of close relationship (typically though not necessarily a marriage) then it must take reasonable steps to satisfy itself that the wife's consent is a free and informed consent. Otherwise, the wife may be able to plead against the bank the misrepresentations or threats of her husband. But what are the 'reasonable steps' which are needed for the bank to be protected?

In *Forsyth* v *Royal Bank of Scotland plc* 2000 SCLR 61 Elizabeth and Henry Forsyth were co-owners of 18 Churchill Drive, Bridge of Allan. Mr Forsyth wished to borrow money in connection with his business as a haulage con-tractor. For this purpose they both granted a standard security to the bank, recorded GRS 6 August 1990. Subsequently, Mrs Forsyth sought reduction, one of the grounds being that her husband had induced her to sign by mis-representation.

Apart from the factual question as to what had taken place between husband and wife, the bank pled that in any event the security could not be voidable as against them, because Mrs Forsyth had been advised by solicitors before she signed. Her response to that was that they were not her solicitors but her husband's solicitors, and also the bank's solicitors, and in those circumstances they could not have given her independent advice. The bank's response was that, whether they were her solicitors or not, they were solicitors and had advised her and they, the bank, were entitled to assume that the advice had been properly given, and to assume that if there had been any conflict of interest the solicitors would have told Mrs Forsyth to seek advice elsewhere.

This precise point has not been litigated before in Scotland, not surprisingly, since this whole area is a new import from a certain country to the south. But in that country the courts have held, in cases of this sort, in favour of the bank. In the present case, English authority was extensively canvassed and the English position adopted. Mrs Forsyth's action was dismissed.

In these 'surety wife' cases the wife holds a gun with two barrels. One barrel is aimed at the bank. It may strike home or (as here) it may not. But she has the other barrel and that barrel is aimed at the law firm which advised her. (We would point out that even before Mrs Forsyth's action against the bank had been dismissed she had already raised an action against the law firm.)

We have had occasion in the past to urge upon solicitors the difficulty they are in when a potential surety wife enters the waiting room. If they agree to advise her, then that will normally prevent her repudiating liability as against the bank, but by the same token the fact that she is liable to the bank means that if that liability is enforced she has a loss which she will be tempted to seek to recoup against the law firm on the ground of negligence.

At first sight, this may not seem such a big risk, for the law firm should simply take care not to give negligent advice. But the risk is bigger than it seems, for the English courts are pitching at extraordinarily high levels the standard of care required of law firms advising 'surety wives'. (For details see an article by Professor Gretton at 1999 SLT 53.) The task of showing that proper advice was indeed given becomes doubly difficult if in fact the law firm in question was acting for the husband or the bank.

## Standard securities and European law

Both European Union law and Human Rights law are liable nowadays to crop up anywhere. In the English case of *Citibank International plc* v *Kessler* [1999] 2 CMLR 603, a German businessman wanted to move back to Germany but was having difficulty selling his house because of structural problems plus a boundary dispute. So he decided to let the house while these problems were resolved. But his lender refused permission. Herr Kessler argued that the clause in the mortgage forbidding any tenancy (equivalent to our Standard Condition 6) had the effect of preventing him from moving within the EU to pursue his business and was therefore a breach of the guaranteed freedom of movement of workers with the EU. The argument failed in the Court of Appeal. It is difficult, however, not to have some sympathy with Herr Kessler. Perhaps Standard Condition 6 is something which needs to be drawn specifically to the attention of clients?

## Descriptions in standard securities

Note 1 of Sched 2 to the Conveyancing and Feudal Reform (Scotland) Act 1970 provides that:

> The security subjects shall be described by means of a particular description or by reference to a description thereof as in Schedule D to the Conveyancing (Scotland) Act 1924 or as in Schedule (G) to the Titles to Land Consolidation (Scotland) Act 1868.

Note 1 applies only to Sasine transactions and first registrations. Once a property is on the Land Register it is both necessary, and also sufficient, to refer to the title number.

In *Beneficial Bank plc* v *McConnachie* 1996 SC 119 the effect of note 1 was said to be that a *particular* description (either directly or by reference) was required in all standard securities. A general description would not do. Accordingly, a standard security which described a terraced house only by its postal address ('the Heritable

Subjects known as 57 Longdykes Road, Prestonpans, in the County of East Lothian') failed to satisfy the requirements of note 1.

This is an awkward rule, and one which does not apply to other conveyancing deeds, such as dispositions. Of course, in most cases, a standard security does in fact contain a particular description, usually by reference. But there is a difficulty with tenement flats. What counts as a particular description of a flat? An answer, of sorts, was given in *Beneficial Bank*. With an upper flat it is sufficient to give its location within the building (*eg* 'top flat south'). But with a flat on the ground floor it is necessary to stipulate the boundaries. The reason for the difference is not fully explained.

In practice, of course, ground floor flats have tended to be described in exactly the same way as other flats. The effect of *Beneficial Bank*, therefore, was to make a large number of securities over ground floor flats ineffective. And for new securities, it became necessary to give a bounding description, whether in words or by plan.

The decision was criticised—see, *eg Professor McDonald's Conveyancing Manual* (6th edn, 1997) para 8.11. But relief is now at hand. Tucked away in the Abolition of Feudal Tenure etc (Scotland) Bill—in para 32(23)(a) of Sched 10—is a new version of note 1 which is to replace the current version. The new version says simply

> The security subjects shall be described sufficiently to identify them; but this note is without prejudice to any additional requirement imposed as respects any register.

The effect of this amendment is to readmit general descriptions. By s 75(1) and (2) of the Bill, the amendment is to come into force immediately on royal assent, likely to be this summer. And by s 75(3) it is retrospective, and so applies to existing securities.

# REAL BURDENS

## Interpretation

Earlier we mentioned *Axis West Developments Ltd* v *Chartwell* 1999 SLT 1416, a decision of the House of Lords giving a rather benevolent interpretation to a deed of servitude. But real burdens fare less well, as a new decision of the First Division shows. In *Heritage Fisheries Ltd* v *Duke of Roxburghe* 1999 GWD 24–1161 it fell to the court to interpret a deed of conditions. The deed, which dated from 1995, sought to regulate maintenance of the Kelso Cauld, an ancient dam on the River Tweed. In essence, the plan was that the western section was to be maintained by the Duke of Roxburghe and the eastern section by Heritage Fisheries.

In the view of the court, the deed was a failure:

> Presumably, the parties hoped and intended that the deed would define their legal relationship clearly and in a manner which would minimise the room for mis-understandings or disputes. In fact, it was drafted in language which is at once obscure and infelicitous and which seems calculated to maximise the scope for

misunderstandings and disputes. All that the court can do in such a situation is to try
to descry from this unsatisfactory language what the parties' intention was.

But such interpretation was not to be even-handed. The deed would be interpreted
*contra proferentem*. When in doubt, the interpretation chosen would be that which
imposed the lighter burden. There was a presumption for freedom.

The particular dispute arose out of the freezing of the river in January 1996,
which caused a breach in the Duke's section of the dam. Was the Duke liable to
repair the breach and restore the dam to its previous condition? That depended
on the proper interpretation of the following clause from the deed of conditions:

> Following the completion of works to the Western Section described under Sub-clause
> Third above, the Duke shall thereafter be responsible for the whole maintenance costs
> of the Western Section as he thinks fit or as may be necessary to comply with the
> aforementioned 1994 Regulations. No alteration to the level of the crest and sides of
> the Kelso Cauld along any part of the Western Section shall be permitted unless with
> the prior consent of the Company.

The crucial question was the meaning of 'maintenance'. (In the context of the
deed as a whole, the court was prepared to interpret the clause as imposing an
obligation to carry out maintenance, rather than merely an obligation to pay for
it.) This was said to be ambiguous. It might mean no more than repair, as the
obligant saw fit. Or it might mean preserve something in its original state, a
higher standard. Which should apply?

> Applying the presumption in favour of freedom, irrespective of any other indications
> from the context, we should require to interpret any real condition as imposing at
> most an obligation to repair. But in any event the context supports that interpretation
> of 'maintenance', since the Duke's obligation is qualified by the words 'as he thinks
> fit or as may be necessary to comply with the aforementioned 1994 Regulations'.

The interpretation seems correct. But there is perhaps some tension between the
view that the court 'should require' to adopt the less onerous meaning, and the
view, stated earlier, that it should 'try to descry . . . what the parties' intention
was'? What would be the position if, while the clause was ambiguous, the more
natural meaning was also the more onerous one?

The presumption for freedom was also used with reference to the final sentence
of the clause. This too was said to be ambiguous. It might impose an obligation
to maintain the crest and sides at their level at the time of the deed (which, following
the damage, was no longer the case). Or it might do no more than restrict the
ambit of any alterations planned by the Duke, and so not apply to alterations
caused by nature. Again, the less onerous interpretation was followed, but again,
this was the interpretation most readily supported by the actual wording.

The end result was that the Duke was found not to be liable. One final point
may be made. The maintenance obligation was cast partly in terms of the '1994
Regulations'. In a well-known case, *Aberdeen Varieties Ltd* v *James F Donald (Aberdeen
Cinemas) Ltd* 1939 SC 788, a real burden was held to be invalid on the basis, *inter
alia*, that it referred to an Act of Parliament without quoting the terms of the Act.
This was said to offend against the rule that the full terms of the burden must

appear in the deed, and hence on the register. If that is really the law, then it is frequently breached in practice (*eg* by maintenance obligations which refer to rateable value). In its forthcoming report on real burdens, the Scottish Law Commission may recommend that the rule be discarded. (The issue is discussed at paras 7.69 and 7.70 of the Commission's *Discussion Paper on Real Burdens* (Scot. Law Com. DP No 106, 1998).) But in any event, the point was not taken in the *Heritage Fisheries* case.

### Title to enforce

*Marsden v Craighelen Lawn Tennis and Squash Club* 1999 GWD 37–1820 concerned the enforceability of a restriction contained in a disposition of 1927 in favour of a tennis club in Helensburgh. The restriction was that:

> the subjects hereinbefore disponed shall be used by the said disponees as Tennis Courts only and under the further condition that there shall be no play thereon on Sundays . . .

The restriction was declared to be a real burden, but no provision was made as to title to enforce.

The litigation concerned a possible breach of the restriction. The club wished to re-develop their facilities, and one result appeared to be that they would cease to be used exclusively for tennis. The pursuers, who were neighbours, sought to enforce the restriction.

The decision covered a number of matters, but only two need be mentioned here. The first concerned title to enforce. The 1927 deed was a disposition and not a feu disposition, so there was no superior. Where, then, did title to enforce lie? This raises one of the most difficult, and least understood, issues in the law of real burdens.

The subjects disponed in 1927 were broken off from larger subjects, extending to more than an acre. For the time being these were retained by the disponer, but later they were divided up and sold as a number of separate properties. The pursuers were owners of various of these properties.

It was argued for the pursuers that where A dispones to B imposing real burdens, the benefited property in such burdens is whatever land may have been reserved by A (if any). That appeared to be the result of the leading case on this subject, *J A Mactaggart & Co v Harrower* (1906) 8 F 1101. From this it would follow that the benefited property in the present case was the one acre or so reserved by the granter of the 1927 disposition. The pursuers were owners of part of that reserved property. Accordingly they had title to sue.

In a long and careful judgment the Sheriff rejected this argument. In his view, there was one crucial difference from the facts of *Mactaggart*. In *Mactaggart*, when the original disponer came to sell the retained land, he expressly assigned the right to enforce the real burden. No such express assignation occurred in the present case. Therefore, there was no right to enforce.

The Sheriff's rule seems to be this. An implied right to enforce a real burden arises where (1) A dispones to B imposing real burdens, (2) A does not sell everything, but reserves some land, *and* (3) when A comes to sell that land, or any part thereof, he expressly assigns the right to enforce the burdens. The novelty here is, of course, (3).

With the greatest respect, however, the Sheriff's decision seems to work neither in theory nor in practice.

It does not work in theory because it muddies the distinction between *contractual* restrictions and *real* burdens. The benefit of a contractual restriction does not run with any land. If it is to transmit, it must be assigned. By contrast, the right to enforce a real burden is, by its very nature, tied to a piece of land (or, in the case of feudal burdens, to the superiority). If the land changes hands then so, automatically, does the right to enforce the burden. Here, real burdens behave in exactly the same way as servitudes. The effect of the Sheriff's decision, if correct, would be to set up a special category of real burden which would not behave in the same way as all other real burdens.

As a historical matter, the issue of assigning real burdens has been a muddle. There are two sorts of real burdens. One is the pecuniary real burden, which is a (now obsolete) form of heritable security. A pecuniary real burden is assignable, like other heritable securities. The other sort of real burden is a real condition affecting land for the benefit of other property (which itself can be a superiority). A real burden in this sense is a *pertinent* of the benefited property, just like a servitude, and does not need to be assigned, for it passes automatically, as a pertinent when the property changes hands. Indeed, the assignation of a real burden (in the second sense) would be without effect.

The Sheriff's decision causes problems in practice also. If the disponer does not sell the retained land for 50 years, the owner of the potentially burdened property will not know for all this period whether the restrictions imposed are contractual or real burdens. The choice remains with the owner of the retained land. If, when he comes to sell, he assigns the right to enforce, the restrictions, at that point, become real burdens. If he fails to assign, the restrictions are still-born and can no longer be enforced. An obvious problem occurs if the original purchaser sells during this initial 50-year period. Is an incoming purchaser bound? If the burdens are real, the answer is yes. If they are contractual, the answer is no. It is difficult to imagine that the answer depends on whether or not the disponer has had the chance to sell on, assigning the right to the burdens.

There are other difficulties. What happens if the first transfer of the retained property is not a voluntary disposition? For example, the owner might die, or be sequestrated. In such a case there will be no assignation in the confirmation or, as the case may be, act and warrant. Does this mean that the real burden fails? Or are universal successors in a different position from singular successors?

It is not clear from the Sheriff's judgment whether future assignations are also required. What happens, for example, if A dispones the retained land to C, assigning enforcement rights, C later dispones to D, assigning enforcement rights, and D later dispones to E without an assignation? Who can enforce? E? D? No one? And if future assignations *are* required, a person acquiring the retained property could be sure of his position only by checking back through each and every disposition. How this would work under registration of title is not clear.

In our opinion the decision of the Sheriff is, with great respect, incorrect. But this is not to defend the rule in *Mactaggart*. Rather the objection is that the decision makes a bad rule even worse. In truth, the rule is bad enough already. In its *Discussion Paper on Real Burdens* (Scot. Law Com. DP No 106, 1998, para 3.19) the Scottish Law Commission pointed out how difficult the rule can be to operate in practice:

> [The rule] requires an exhaustive investigation into the position of the granter at the time of the original grant. Enquiries must be made as to whether he owned other property in the neighbourhood, and, if so, the details must be retrieved. Often the information is difficult to come by. If the granter owned a substantial estate, it will be necessary to trace other grants made out of the same estate in order to determine how much of the estate was left at the material time. The subsequent history of this residual dominant tenement must then be investigated. Often the tenement will have come to be divided up, perhaps into many different parts, and if so each constituent part continues to form a dominant tenement in the burden, and the consent of its current owner must be obtained for any waiver.

In its forthcoming final report on real burdens, the Commission may recommend that all enforcement rights arising under the *Mactaggart* rule are extinguished, unless positive steps are taken to save them by registering, within a limited period (say 10 years), a notice of preservation. This uses the technique already used for saving certain rights of superiors under the Abolition of Feudal Tenure (Scotland) Bill.

One other aspect of *Marsden* is worth mentioning. One of the restrictions imposed was a prohibition against playing tennis on a Sunday. That, said the Sheriff, could not be a real burden. A real burden must confer praedial benefit, *ie* benefit on a person in his capacity as owner of property. The benefit here was purely personal in character. This conclusion seems open to question. A prohibition on play on a Sunday might be more than sabbatarianism. The area surrounding the tennis courts was of a residential nature. Tennis can be a noisy activity. Owners tend to be at home at the weekends. A prohibition on play on one of the weekend days preserves peace and quiet, and hence general amenity. That seems just as praedial as, say, the traditional prohibition on the boiling-up of horses.

## INSOLVENCY AND SPECIAL DESTINATIONS

We deal with these two topics together here, since the new decision on special destinations is also a bankruptcy case.

### Does a trustee in sequestration acquire a real right without registration?

When a person is sequestrated, his property 'vests' in the trustee in sequestration: that is elementary. But what is the exact nature of the vesting? Should the trustee complete title in his own name? If he does not, is it necessary (in Sasine cases) to deduce title when he sells? What if the property has still not been sold when the debtor is discharged, which normally happens three years after the sequestration? This latter question is of considerable practical importance, for it is a situation of frequent occurrence. (Why? We don't know. In 1999 alone there are two reported examples, namely *Souter* v *Kennedy* and *Fleming's Tr* v *Fleming*, both discussed below.)

In our view the following principles (given here only in summary form) operate:

(1)  The statutory vesting does not, of itself, give to the trustee in sequestration any real right in the heritable property.

(2)  Thus the debtor remains legally the owner, unless and until either (a) the trustee sells, or (b) the trustee completes title in his own name.

(3)  Following on from the above, a trustee in sequestration is free to complete a title in his own name. (Not, of course, for his own benefit, but as trustee for the creditors.) In a Sasine case he will do this by means of a notice of title.

(4)  If the trustee does not complete title in his own name before selling, he probably needs to deduce title in the disposition, the midcouple being the act and warrant. (Not necessary, of course, in Land Register cases.)

(5)  If title remains in the debtor by the time of his discharge (normally three years after the date of sequestration) the property remains subject to the sequestration. The trustee can still complete title and sell. Alternatively, he can still sell without having completed title, just as if the debtor had not been discharged.

(6)  However, in the situation described in (5), the trustee in sequestration ought to register in the Register of Inhibitions and Adjudications a notice of renewal conform to s 14(4) of the Bankruptcy (Scotland) Act 1985. If he fails to do this (and if he also has not completed title in his own name) then a risk emerges: the risk that the debtor will himself sell the property. If that happens, the title of the buyer will not be affected by the sequestration. This is laid down by s 44(4) (as amended) of the Conveyancing (Scotland) Act 1924. In other words, a trustee in sequestration should, before the debtor is discharged, either (a) sell, or (b) complete title in his own name, or (c) register a notice of renewal.

*Souter* v *Kennedy* (23 July 1999, Perth Sheriff Court, not yet reported) is a good illustration of the sort of problems that can arise in this area, though the specific facts of the case were unusual. Mr X was sequestrated in 1983. Mr Kennedy was appointed as trustee in sequestration. Mr X was later discharged, but financial success was not written in his stars, for in 1996 he was sequestrated again. This time the trustee in sequestration was Mr Souter. At the time of his sequestration in 1983 Mr X owned certain heritable property. Mr Kennedy did not sell this. Nor did he complete title in his own name. Nor, it seems, did he record any notices of renewal. (The 1983 sequestration was, of course, subject to the Bankruptcy (Scotland) Act 1913, but similar principles applied under that Act.) After the second sequestration, Mr Souter noted that the debtor had a title to the property in question. Mr Souter completed title to this property in his own name.

Mr Souter and Mr Kennedy were thus both in the position of wishing to sell the property for the benefit of creditors, Mr Souter for the benefit of the creditors in the 1996 sequestration and Mr Kennedy for the benefit of the creditors in the 1983 sequestration. To resolve the issue, Mr Souter raised an action of declarator to the effect that he was now the heritable proprietor and that he would have the sole right to the proceeds of sale. The Sheriff found in favour of Mr Kennedy. The pursuer appealed to the Sheriff Principal, who refused the appeal. It is understood that the pursuer is to appeal to the Inner House of the Court of Session.

The reasoning in the case is too long and technical for discussion here. But in brief it seems to have been held that the act and warrant in the 1983 sequestration created a real right in favour of Mr Kennedy. With respect, we think that that cannot be correct. Subject to certain known exceptions (such as servitudes) a real right in heritable property cannot come into being without registration in the Sasine Register or Land Register (as appropriate). That is a pretty basic principle of Scots property law. There exists a strong presumption that statutory provisions are not to be construed as violating that basic principle. It is true that the vesting provisions in the 1913 Act are rather odd—and there are also some oddities in the equivalent provisions in the 1985 Act. But one must not allow the tail to wag the dog. Hitherto, these vesting provisions have never been interpreted in the way asserted on behalf of the defender. In another 1999 case, *Fleming's Tr v Fleming* (see below) Lord Caplan remarked that:

> 'In terms of s 31(1)(b) of the 1985 Act the permanent trustee by virtue of his act and warrant acquires the right of an adjudger holding a decree of adjudication. The effect of such an adjudication is of course to confer a *personal* right upon which infeftment may proceed.' (Emphasis added.)

We would respectfully agree with Lord Caplan's remark. We see here no difference between the 1913 Act and the 1985 Act.

The learned Sheriff Principal relies much on some *dicta* of Lord Inglis in *Heritable Reversionary Co v Millar (McKay's Tr)* when that celebrated case was in the Court of Session ((1891) 18 R 1166). In those *dicta*, Lord Inglis stressed that the applicable statute at the time (Bankruptcy (Scotland) Act 1856) conferred 'as comprehensive a title as any statute could possibly confer'. But we would suggest it is perfectly possible to agree with Lord Inglis without drawing the conclusion reached by the learned Sheriff Principal. In the case which was before Lord Inglis the party claiming as against the trustee in sequestration *had no real right*. By contrast, Mr Souter had a completed title. The issues were thus of an entirely different nature, and accordingly one must understand the *dicta* of Lord Inglis in the context in which they were pronounced. We thus incline to the view that the appeal should succeed.

It may be worth concluding by examining the matter from the practical standpoint of a third party who wishes to buy. Suppose that a debtor has been discharged from his sequestration, and suppose that certain heritable property has not been sold by the trustee, and also that the trustee has not completed a title to it, so that the title remains in the debtor. And suppose that a third party wishes to buy the property. Whom should he approach to grant the disposition? The law seems to be that *either* the trustee *or* the debtor can grant a valid disposition of the property, each without the consent of the other. The trustee can grant a disposition because the property still forms part of the sequestrated estate and the discharge of the debtor does not restore his property to him. The debtor can grant a disposition by a combination of two facts: (a) that he is still infeft, and (b) s 44 of the Conveyancing (Scotland) Act 1924. However, it should be stressed that the debtor's power to dispone will be excluded if the trustee has timeously recorded a notice of renewal. However, whilst the foregoing appears to be the law we would admit, from a practical standpoint, to a sense of nervousness at the idea of taking a title from the debtor alone.

### Special destinations and bankruptcy

Back in 1951 Lord President Cooper said (*Hay's Tr* v *Hay's Trs* 1951 SC 329):

> It seems to me unfortunate that the device of a special destination, originally introduced before 1868 for the purpose of overcoming the prohibition which then prevailed against wills of heritage, should still be utilised in circumstances which, as our reports show, are more likely to be productive of litigation than of any compensating advantage to the parties concerned.

Those words have been echoed by many judges since, and yet the conveyancing profession has been slow to take note. Inevitably, the litigation has continued.

*Fleming's Tr* v *Fleming* 2000 SLT 406 (IH) deals with the following situation. A and B are co-owners of a house with a survivorship destination. One of them dies, insolvent. Does the survivor take the half share, or do the creditors? And if she takes the half share is she then liable to the creditors for its value?

This issue was litigated in a case called *Barclays Bank* v *McGreish* 1983 SLT 344, in which Lord Stott held that the survivor would take the property and have no liability to the creditors. That case provoked a snowstorm of debate: see Cusine 1984 JLSS 154, Morton 1984 SLT (News) 133, Halliday 1984 SLT (News) 180 and Gretton 1984 SLT (News) 299. Of these only Halliday defended the decision, but he later changed his mind: see his *Conveyancing Law and Practice* (2nd edn, 1997) para 22–18 (para 49–18 of the 1st edn). The decision thus looked weak. It has now at last been overruled.

The facts of *Fleming's Tr* were as follows. Thomas and Elizabeth Fleming were co-owners of 24 Cochart Avenue, Coatbridge. The title contained a survivorship destination. Thomas was sequestrated in 1990 and discharged after the normal three-year period, in 1993. He died in 1995. By the time of his death the trustee in sequestration had, it seems, neither completed title to the half share nor taken any steps to realise it. After Thomas's death the trustee raised an action against Elizabeth. In it he sought, in the alternative, either:

(a) declarator that the effect of the sequestration was to knock out the destination so that on Thomas's death his half share did not pass to his widow,

or, *esto* the declaratory conclusion was unsuccessful, then:

(b) decree against Elizabeth for payment to the trustee of the fair value of the half share which had passed to her under the destination.

The Extra Division held against the trustee on the first point but in his favour on the second.

On the first point, there was some room for doubt, because the whole doctrine of what is sometimes called 'automatic infeftment' is at bottom an incoherent one. (The case which introduced the doctrine, *Bisset v Walker* 26 Nov 1799 Fac Coll, was wrongly decided but, of course, it is too late to question it now.) Being incoherent it is difficult to argue about it in a principled way, but the approach of the Division is a sensible one. If the trustee in sequestration had completed title to Thomas's half share then the destination would have been evacuated, but it was open to argument whether evacuation could occur by the mere fact of sequestration. The position of a trustee in sequestration who has not completed a title in his own name is rather like that of a person who has received a disposition but not registered it. Suppose that Thomas had, before his death, granted a disposition to X but that X had not completed title. Would the destination still take effect? Whilst there is (we believe) no express authority on this point, there can surely be little doubt that the destination would still operate. (X might then have had a personal claim against Thomas's estate, of course.)

On the second point, there seems no doubt. When title is taken to A whom failing B, A is the 'institute' and B is the 'substitute' or, to use a term which means the same, the 'heir of provision'. In a survivorship destination to A and B, what is happening is that one half is disponed to A whom failing to B and the other half is disponed to B whom failing to A. Each is thus institute of his original half share and substitute of the other half share. Once expressed in this traditional terminology, the result is obvious from the old authorities. For the old authorities say expressly that an heir of provision who 'takes' under the destination can be made liable, by the unpaid creditors of the institute, to the extent of the value (*ad valorem*) of the property which has passed. So Elizabeth was liable up to the value of the half share which she took.

That left two loose ends to tie up. One was whether the fact that Thomas had been discharged was relevant. It was held that it was not, and this decision too seems correct. As has been mentioned earlier, the discharge of a person from his sequestration does not normally have any effect on property which was vested in the trustee but not yet disposed of, and this is so even if the trustee has not completed title. One exception which was mentioned earlier is s 44(4) of the Conveyancing (Scotland) Act 1924 (as amended). It is doubtful whether it could have applied in this case, but at all events it seems not to have been pled.

The other loose end was whether an action should have been at the instance of the creditors themselves, rather than at the instance of the trustee in sequestration. Here, the court had no difficulty in deciding, surely correctly, that the trustee did indeed have title to sue.

Finally, *Fleming's Tr* contains some interesting *obiter dicta* from Lord Caplan on that celebrated case which launched a thousand articles, *Sharp v Thomson*:

In *Sharp* v *Thomson* 1995 SC 455 (in the Inner House) the Lord President gave an exhaustive and learned analysis of the distinction between real and personal property. A real right is a right which attaches to the property and is apt to be valid against the whole world. On the other hand a personal right is an aspect of the law of inter-personal obligations and its effect does not extend beyond the persons affected by it. These rights cannot be fragmented. There is no intermediate right between a real right and a personal right. In the House of Lords (1997 SC(HL) 66) the Inner House was overturned on a speciality relating to the legislation governing floating charges but the Lord President's analysis of the general rights affecting property was not attacked. The effect of *Sharp* was to reinforce the traditional approach of Scots Law that registration in the public records is the key to the creation and ranking of real rights in Scotland.

That is an approach with which we are, respectfully, in general agreement.

# REGISTRATION OF TITLE

## Rectification

The theory of registration of title is that, once on the Register, you are there for good. Defects in the conveyancing no longer matter. Title flows from the Register and not from the deeds. By the same token, if you are buying from someone with a registered title, you are entitled to rely on what you find on the Register, and do not need to go behind the Register and examine the prior deeds. In fact, there would be little point in registration of title if you had to conduct a full Sasine-type examination of title.

But what if the Register is, in fact, inaccurate? What if the Keeper has made an entry which was not justified by the deed which you (or a predecessor) presented to him? It is easy to think of examples. The deed might have been forged, or improperly signed, or granted by the wrong person, or by a person without legal capacity; or the whole transaction might be reducible as a gratuitous alienation, or a fraudulent preference, or as designed to defeat the financial claims of a spouse, or as a breach of some previous contract.

The theory is supposed to be that such an inaccuracy makes no difference. You can still rely on the Register. Registration is absolution. (Later, however, we discuss a challenge to this view.) The legislative basis of this protection is s 9 of the Land Registration (Scotland) Act 1979. The scheme of the Act appears to be that, except where the registered proprietor consents (as, for example, when he sells the property to someone else), the Register can be altered only by an application for rectification, under s 9. But s 9(3) then restricts the circumstances in which rectification is allowed. The Register can be rectified against a proprietor in possession only in very limited circumstances, most notably (i) where he has caused the inaccuracy by his fraud or carelessness or (ii) where the Keeper has excluded indemnity. Needless to say the Keeper does not often exclude indemnity, and we can leave this case aside. What s 9(3) means, for the ordinary owner, is that he is safe provided only that he is in possession and has not been fraudulent or careless.

## Meaning of 'carelessness'

The strength of this protection depends to some extent on what is meant by 'careless'. (It can be assumed that we know what is meant by fraud.) In the first 20 years of land registration this has remained something of a mystery. But two cases decided in 1999 cast some light on the word.

The more extended discussion is in *Wilson* v *Keeper of the Registers of Scotland* 2000 SLT 267, 1999 SCLR 872. Here a title presented for first registration was argued to have been to some extent invalid. If so, no one had noticed. The full deeds were before both the solicitors for the purchasers (who were the applicants for first registration) and also the Keeper. Had there been carelessness by the purchasers, who were now proprietors in possession? In the event, the issue was not explored, but Lord McCluskey offered some comments of a general nature (p 887):

> [A]s we are dealing with a matter of carelessness in a very special context, it would, in our opinion, be important for the appellants to explain what standard of care it was sought to be applied. The importance of this may be seen in *Hunter* v *Hanley* 1955 SC 200. In a matter of the present kind, where any carelessness would apparently have to be on the part of the solicitors rather than the actual proprietor in possession, there would evidently have to be material indicating that the solicitors departed from a usual and normal professional practice, or that the alleged failure to discover alleged flaws in the title . . . was a failure which no professional conveyancer of ordinary skill would have committed if acting with ordinary care.

*Hunter* v *Hanley* is, of course, a leading case on professional negligence; and Lord McCluskey appears to be treating 'carelessness' as meaning much the same as 'negligence'—perhaps a rather narrow interpretation. (After all, if negligence had been intended, it would have been easy for the statute to use the word.) This interpretation, if correct, is quite a convenient one for the proprietor in possession. If his solicitor has not been negligent, then he (the proprietor) cannot be dislodged by rectification. But if the solicitor has been negligent, and the proprietor has been dislodged, then the very evidence which justifies rectification also justifies a claim against the solicitor for professional negligence. (The 'carelessness' would of course prevent a claim for indemnity against the Keeper: see s 12(3)(n).)

Another factor which may be of relevance is foreseeability. This point was emphasised in *Dougbar Properties Ltd* v *Keeper of the Registers of Scotland* 1999 SC 513, 1999 SCLR 458. For an act or omission to be 'careless', according to Lord Macfadyen, it must be one which is reasonably foreseeably likely to result in an inaccuracy in the Register (see pp 532–533).

Both analyses are (and are intended to be) provisional and incomplete. But they are at any rate a start.

## Who can apply?

Who can apply for rectification? On this the 1979 Act is silent. Section 9(1) merely empowers the Keeper to rectify 'whether on being so requested or not'. There is no indication of who has the right to make the request. The decision of the Inner

House in *Wilson* v *Keeper of the Registers of Scotland* 2000 SLT 267, 1999 SCLR 872 suggests that the application must be made by the person who is to gain directly from the rectification which is being proposed.

In that case, the application was to have the owner of certain property changed from X, the current owner, to Y. Y was a trustee. The application, however, was made, not by Y, but by potential beneficiaries under the trust of which Y was trustee. (It was a public trust and there was a wide class of beneficiary.) It was held that there was no entitlement to apply for rectification. Only Y could apply. The person whose name it was proposed to put on the Register must be the applicant. Otherwise a person could find himself as owner (and subject to potential liabilities) without his knowledge or even against his will. This, according to the court, was shown even more clearly by considering the normal alternative to rectification, which was payment of indemnity. Only Y, the allegedly displaced owner, could apply for indemnity, for only Y had suffered loss. But if that were so, only Y could apply for rectification. We would agree with this approach. It is a traditional principle of property law that a person cannot lose ownership without his consent (the *animus transferendi dominii*) and equally that he cannot acquire ownership without his consent (the *animus accipiendi dominii*). There are exceptions, indeed, but that is the principle, and it is a good one.

### Prospective not retrospective

If rectification is actually obtained, it does not operate retrospectively. That point has now been settled both by *Stevenson-Hamilton's Exrs* v *McStay* 1999 SLT 1175 and by *M R S Hamilton Ltd* v *Keeper of the Registers of Scotland* 2000 SLT 352. Any other result would indeed have been surprising. Thus, suppose (as was alleged to have happened in *Stevenson-Hamilton*) that Alice, in year 1, grants to Brendan a disposition of land which actually belongs to Zelda. Brendan then applies for registration in the Land Register. The Keeper may refuse, but suppose that for one reason or another he accepts, and Brendan is registered. Although the disposition is *a non domino*, the effect of registration is to make Brendan the owner. (See s 3(1)(a) of the 1979 Act.) This is because title flows from the Register and not from the underlying deeds. Suppose further that, in year 6, Zelda brings a successful application for rectification. As a result, Brendan's name is deleted from the proprietorship section, and Zelda's name is inserted. But the change is not retrospective. Zelda becomes owner only in year 6, and Brendan—though he should not have been there in the first place—is acknowledged as owner for the whole period that he was on the Register (years 1 to 5).

### Registration

Rectification is limited by s 9(3) of the 1979 Act. But whilst a proprietor in possession is protected against *rectification* he is not protected against *registration*. One way of looking at it is to say that the Land Register has two doors, the front door, marked 'registration' and the side door marked 'rectification'. The side door (rectification) is very difficult to get through. But the front door (registration) is wide open. Usually, of course, registration follows on from the voluntary act of the registered owner (*eg* the grant of a disposition or standard security). But not always. In cases where registration is not consented to but is competent, the registered owner will lose his property, despite the fact that he is in possession.

As already mentioned, the 1979 Act may well have been drafted on the basis that, where the Register is inaccurate and hence where rectification is available (at least in principle), rectification *must* be employed, and registration is not competent. The availability of one door (albeit subject to severe restrictions) excludes the use of the other. However, that view has been persistently challenged in the long-running litigation involving the trustee in sequestration of Alexander Short.

The facts here are probably familiar to most readers. Mr Short sold two flats in Great George Street, in Glasgow, to a Mr Chung at substantially below market value. Mr Chung disponed the flats to his wife without payment. Mrs Chung was entered on the Register as proprietor. All this took place back in October 1986. There has been more or less constant litigation ever since. There have been three phases of litigation. Each phase involved the case going to the Inner House. In the second stage it went all the way up to the House of Lords.

**Stage One.** The first thing that happened was that Mr Short was sequestrated. His trustee then sought reduction of the various dispositions, as gratuitous alienations. That litigation went to the Second Division (*Short's Tr* v *Chung* 1991 SLT 472). The trustee prevailed, and the dispositions were reduced.

**Stage Two.** The question then arose as to how to get the reductions into the Land Register. The obvious route was to apply for rectification. But Mrs Chung was a proprietor in possession and was not in bad faith. Hence, she was protected by s 9(3) of the 1979 Act. So the trustee had the idea of applying not for rectification but for registration instead—as, indeed, would be normal practice for Sasine titles. The Keeper refused this application as incompetent. The trustee litigated all the way to the House of Lords, but lost all the way: see *Short's Tr* v *Keeper of the Registers of Scotland* 1996 SC(HL) 14. (For some discussion of this stage of the litigation see Professor Reid's article at 1996 *Scottish Law and Practice Quarterly* 265.)

**Stage Three.** But the trustee was not finished. The decree of reduction had, in the event, done him little good. So back he went to court and asked instead for an order ordaining Mrs Chung to grant a disposition in his favour, within 28 days. In other words, in place of a reduction, he sought a conveyance. The reason is apparent. Whatever may be the position about reductions, there can at any rate be no doubt that a disposition can always enter the Register by registration. Hence, if he could get a disposition the trustee should be home and dry. The fact that Mrs Chung was a proprietor in possession would no longer matter.

At first instance, the trustee's action was successful: *Short's Tr* v *Chung* (No 2) 1997 SCLR 1181, 1998 SC 105, 1998 SLT 200. Mrs Chung appealed. The appeal has failed. The decision of the Inner House is reported at 1999 SLT 751. So far as we are aware, there is to be no further appeal.

The full significance of this decision is hard to assess. It may come to be interpreted narrowly (*eg* as confined to gratuitous alienations). Or it might be reconsidered by a later court on the basis that it was not argued on the merits, for the sole issue before the court was the question of *res judicata*. (That issue arose because the trustee in sequestration had previously obtained a decree of reduction, and the argument was that that decree meant that the matter could not be relitigated.) On the other hand, the decision may come to be applied in a wide range of situations. If so, it will damage the system of land registration. It will mean that a purchaser may no longer be able to rely on what he sees on the Register. If the Register turns out to be inaccurate—if, in other words, there is something wrong with one of the earlier deeds—the inaccuracy could lead to an application for a conveyance away from the registered proprietor in favour of the other party in question, the party with the right to challenge. The fact that the purchaser was a proprietor in possession would then be no defence: the fact that the side door (rectification) was locked would make no difference.

A defect in one of the earlier deeds might mean that that deed was (a) void or (b) voidable. The risk to which a voidable deed gives rise is not, in most cases, great. Generally, reduction—or a demand for a conveyance—would not succeed against a purchaser in good faith. In other words, the common law provides a protection not unlike that of s 9(3) of the 1979 Act. (In the specific case of gratuitous alienation, see s 34(4) of the Bankruptcy (Scotland) Act 1985.)

The position may be different if the deed in question is not voidable but void. In such a case a demand for reduction—and by analogy a demand for a conveyance—can be met with no obvious defence. Take the following example. David buys a house from Caroline. Caroline is the registered owner. David registers his disposition and takes entry. He is then the registered owner. Now, suppose that the recent history of the title was this. Caroline had acquired from Brendan and Brendan in turn had acquired from Alice. The disposition from Brendan to Caroline was fine, but that from Alice to Brendan was void, *eg* because granted *a non domino*, or forged. In the Sasine system, the nullity of the initial disposition (Alice to Brendan) would deprive David of all title (at least until positive prescription had run). Under registration of title, David is owner, but the Register is, or may be, inaccurate. In other words, whereas in the Sasine Register D's title would be void, in the Land Register David's title is valid but inaccurate. Following *Short's Tr* v *Chung*, the party with the right to challenge David's title might seek a conveyance from David. The probable ground of action would be unjustified enrichment.

If this sort of possibility is taken seriously, it would suggest that purchasers can no longer rely on the Register but must look behind it at the deeds which gave rise to the current entry. In other words, they must carry out an examination of title, Sasine-style. But, since *positive* prescription does not usually apply to registered titles, the examination would presumably have to go back for the 20 years of the *negative* prescription. Whether the necessary deeds could be obtained is, of course, another matter.

We doubt whether we have really reached that point. A number of factors mitigate the effect of *Short's Tr* v *Chung*.

First, there seems little danger from the fact that a deed is *voidable*, so long at least as the purchaser is in good faith. And the risk from a *void* deed depends on a view of the law of unjustified enrichment which might well prove unsound. In the example given above, David acquired from the then owner, Caroline, and paid the full price. It is difficult to see how David has been enriched.

Second, from this it follows that the risk in practice would be small—too small, probably, to justify making a full examination of prior deeds as a matter of normal conveyancing.

Might the matter be covered by the indemnity scheme? Admittedly that would not be true on the traditional view of indemnity. This would allow payment only if the Register were altered by *rectification* (see s 12(1)(a)). But that view has been challenged. In two recent cases the view was taken that s 12(1)(d) of the Act is sufficiently wide to allow a claim whenever the land certificate (and hence, indirectly, the Register) is inaccurate, even if no rectification has taken place. The cases are *M R S Hamilton Ltd* v *Keeper of the Registers of Scotland* (Lands Tribunal, 19 May 1998), and *M R S Hamilton Ltd* v *Keeper of the Registers of Scotland* (No 1) 1999 SLT 829. But the first case was appealed and on 25 January 2000 the First Division reversed the decision of the Lands Tribunal (2000 SLT 352). That decision, while no doubt correct, makes the position of the registered proprietor a little less secure.

## Indemnity

Now for some good news. If registration of title can sometimes give you less than you deserve, it can also sometimes give you more.

Suppose that, on first registration, the Keeper makes a mistake and gives you greater rights than you ought to get. But this is his fault and not yours. You gave him all the title deeds. You did not mislead him in any way. It is simply that he has been over-generous. You know of his mistake, but he does not. Later he finds out. He rectifies the Register. (He is able to do so because you do not actually have possession of the windfall benefit.) Are you entitled to indemnity for the loss of your windfall?

The answer, according to *Dougbar Properties Ltd* v *Keeper of the Registers of Scotland* 1999 SC 513, 1999 SCLR 458, is yes. The facts there were much as described above, except that the property had been sold on, and indemnity was claimed by the new owners. The owners had been perfectly aware, at the time of acquisition, that the Register conferred an undue windfall. So the eventual rectification came as no surprise. Their claim was for £1.39 million, which is thought to be the highest claim yet made against the Keeper.

Not surprisingly, the claim was resisted by the Keeper. In particular, he argued that (a) there was no real loss, since the claimants knew all along they were not entitled to the right (b) the claimants were 'careless' in applying for registration, or at least in applying without drawing the Keeper's attention to his mistake, and accordingly no indemnity was due (because of s 12(3)(n) of the 1979 Act).

Both arguments were rejected by Lord Macfadyen. Argument (a) seems pretty clearly wrong. One minute the claimants had the right in question. The next minute the Keeper had taken it away from them by rectification. That was clear loss. And the whole principle of land registration is that you have whatever rights the Register says you have—even if (as here) you should not have been given them in the first place.

Argument (b) is less clearcut, but is probably wrong also. It is difficult to see why it should be 'careless' to rely on the Register. The purchasers' private knowledge meant that they knew they were taking a risk that the Register would be rectified; but they also knew that, in the event of rectification taking place, they would be entitled to indemnity. This overall position was part of their calculations on purchase, and was presumably factored into the price paid.

The broad principle of the decision seems correct, as the legislation currently stands. If the Keeper confers rights, he cannot then take them away without paying indemnity. (Whether this is a sensible policy is of course another matter entirely).

Two further points may be mentioned. First, the title was a long lease, and the actual right in question was a right to park on adjacent property leased (from the same landlords) by Asda. But the nature of such a right seems open to question. It was assumed by the court that the right was a real right. But what kind of a real right was not explored. It could not be a servitude, because a mere lessee cannot hold a servitude. Nor was it ownership. Nor does it sound like a lease, since the right was very limited in character. The issue is of more than theoretical importance because if the claimants did not, after all, have a real right, this would greatly reduce their claim for indemnity.

The other is that we are here dealing with two title sheets and not with one. As well as the claimants' title sheet, there was also the Asda title sheet; and while the right of parking was mentioned in the former it was not (presumably) mentioned in the latter. But can Asda be affected by a right which is not included in their title sheet? The 1979 Act suggests not. The effect of Asda's initial registration, according to s 3(1)(a), was to give Asda a real right of lease 'subject only to the effect of any matter entered in the title sheet of the interest . . . and to any overriding interest . . .' But the claimants' right of parking was neither entered in the title sheet nor was it an overriding interest. There is a more fundamental issue lurking here. The Act presupposes that title sheets will not contradict one another, and if they do (as appears to have happened here) the Act offers no resolution.

# SOLICITORS

In *Bristol & West Building Society* v *Aitken Nairn WS* 2000 SCLR 47 (IH) lenders instructed the defenders to take security over 'Feudal Castle, Freswick Castle, Caithness'. That was all. Apparently this was a remortgage. The defenders prepared and recorded a standard security over the *dominium utile*. The borrower (a Mr Newell) later became insolvent, and the proceeds of the sale of the property fell far short of the amount of the loan. The lenders argued that the solicitors were liable to them because they had not disclosed that the barony title had—by a somewhat complex series of conveyancing transactions—been separated from the *dominium utile*, so that the value of the security was lower than it would otherwise have been. The lenders argued that the defenders knew this because they themselves had carried out the conveyancing. At first instance, the action was dismissed on the basis that the defenders had carried out the lenders' instructions. They had indeed obtained for the lenders a security over 'Feudal Castle, Freswick Castle, Caithness'. If the pursuers had wished to have a security which extended to the barony title, they should have said so. That decision has now been reversed, and a proof allowed.

The factual background to the case was obscure when it was at first instance, and whilst certain matters have now become clearer, others remain obscure, and indeed Lord Penrose, in giving the opinion of the Division, comments on the continuing factual obscurity. ('The parties' pleadings show a surprising lack of consensus as to the consequences of the conveyancing which was carried out. The deeds have not been incorporated, and have not been before the court. . .') But leaving that point on one side, the reason for the decision of the Division was that 'the pursuers are entitled to a proof to establish, if they can, that no solicitor could have believed that the sequence of events was of no significance to a lender'. What this seems to boil down to is that the pursuers were entitled to insist that the expression 'Feudal Castle, Freswick Castle, Caithness' should be construed in the light of the whole circumstances of the case: what those circumstances were would be a matter for proof.

Another aspect of the case is that there were inhibitions against Mr Newell which the defenders did not disclose to the lenders, because they were to be discharged at settlement. The pursuers argued that their agents had a duty to disclose the existence of these inhibitions as bearing upon the financial standing of Mr Newell. The opinion of the Division says very little about this aspect of the case. It is not easy to say whether or not a solicitor has a duty to disclose such inhibitions. (Obviously, an inhibition which is not being discharged ought to be disclosed.) Certainly, the cautious approach would be to disclose.

Whilst we would not wish to question the decision of the Division, nevertheless it is difficult not to have considerable sympathy with the robust approach of the Lord Ordinary, which was that the instructions issued by the lenders said nothing at all about any barony title, and that if professional moneylenders cannot take the trouble to issue instructions saying what they mean then they must suffer the consequences. (This is our paraphrase and goes beyond the language actually used by the Lord Ordinary.) What we are seeing here—viewed from an academic standpoint—is the relentless rise of 'good faith' in the interpretation of obligations: the Division is taking a 'good faith' approach. Or, to put the same point in different language, the Division was prepared to read into the instructions implied terms. Of course, it must be stressed that the Division did not hold that the instructions *did* impliedly include an instruction that the security should extend to the barony title. It merely allowed the pursuers to attempt to prove that they did.

The case is of significance for conveyancers, and will, perhaps, not be wholly welcome. They will be liable for breaches of the literal terms of letters of instructions from lenders, but they may also be liable for failing to do what they ought to have known the lenders wanted done, even though not expressed in the letter of instruction.

Another case which is unlikely to bring joy to the hearts of conveyancers is *Leeds & Holbeck Building Society* v *Alex Morison & Co* 1999 GWD 9–434. The facts of this case are not wholly clear, but it appears that when the lenders enforced their security they found that the property was in the process of being converted from a house into a hotel, that this was in breach of the terms of the security, and that the law firm were aware of the intentions of the client but did not inform them. The defenders' position seems to have been that at the time of the advance the property was indeed in residential use, and that they had no duty to disclose what were mere future intentions, being intentions which might, even if carried out, not lead to any breach of the terms of the security. No breach might ensue because the client might apply successfully for a waiver from the lenders, or might refinance the project. The defenders argued that the action was therefore irrelevant. The Lord Ordinary seems to have taken the view that there would be a duty to disclose information about intentions, and allowed a proof apparently on the question of what the agents knew and when they knew it. We have some doubt about the soundness of the decision.

Finally, we would mention that the flood of actions by lenders against law firms continues unabated south of the border. Examples of reported cases from 1999 are *Birmingham Midshires Building Society* v *Infields* (1999) 66 Con LR 20, *Abbey National plc* v *Frost* [1999] 2 All ER 206, and *Paragon Finance plc* v *D B Thakerar & Co* [1999] 1 All ER 400, and of course there have been many unreported cases. A frequent theme is the following. A secured loan is made but the borrower makes no repayments and vanishes. The security is enforced but the price achieved turns out to be much less than the loan. The lender suffers a significant loss, and argues that the solicitor involved knew enough to alert him to the fraud, but failed to disclose what he knew. It has to be conceded that some of the cases one hears about are truly shocking, and it is difficult to have sympathy for the solicitor involved.

We expect the flow of cases of this sort to continue on both sides of the border. It is true that non-disclosure of information about the client's financial affairs is not in itself a breach of duty to the lender, unless, of course, the law firm has been expressly asked to make such disclosure: *cf National Homes Loans* v *Giffen Couch & Archer* [1997] 3 All ER 808. But there is a duty to disclose relevant information about the property itself, including its value: *cf Mortgage Express* v *Bowerman* [1996] 2 All ER 836.

# ABOLITION OF THE FEUDAL SYSTEM

The Abolition of Feudal Tenure etc (Scotland) Bill was introduced to the Scottish Parliament on 6 October 1999 and, following a report by the Justice and Home

Affairs Committee, successfully completed stage 1 (approval in principle) on 15 December 1999. It is expected to complete all its parliamentary stages, and to have received Royal Assent, by June 2000.

The Bill is almost identical to the one prepared by the Scottish Law Commission and published in February 1999 as part of its *Report on Abolition of the Feudal System* (Scot. Law Com. No 168). A full explanation of the Bill will be found in that report. Two summary accounts have also been published, in 1999 SLT (News) 95, and at JLSS 24–26 February 1999.

It is not possible in the space available to give a full account of a Bill which comprises 75 sections and 11 schedules, and which runs to more than 100 pages. But in any case it would be premature, since the Bill will doubtless be further amended during its parliamentary passage. For the moment we do no more than draw attention to its most important features.

## Feudal system to go

That the feudal system is to go is scarcely news. Section 1 of the Bill sets the tone:

> The feudal system of land tenure, that is to say, the entire system whereby land is held by a vassal on perpetual tenure from a superior is, on the appointed day, abolished.

Most of the Bill will come into force on the 'appointed day'. That is the day of feudal abolition and is likely to be a year or two after Royal Assent. But, as we will see, some of the Bill comes into force immediately on Royal Assent.

The detail of feudal abolition is given in s 2:

> 2(1) An estate of *dominium utile* of land shall, on the appointed day, cease to exist as a feudal estate but shall forthwith become the ownership of the land and, in so far as is consistent with the provisions of this Act, the land shall be subject to the same subordinate real rights and other encumbrances as was the estate of *dominium utile*.
>
> 2(2) Every other feudal estate in land shall, on that day, cease to exist.
>
> 2(3) It shall, on that day, cease to be possible to create a feudal estate in land.

## Feuduty to go

Part 3 of the Bill deals with feuduty. By s 7 all remaining feuduties are extinguished on the appointed day. But the former superior has two years to claim compensation by serving a notice in the statutory form (Scheds 1 and 2) on the person who was vassal immediately before the appointed day (s 8). Compensation is calculated by reference to the value of 2.5% Consols, in the usual way (s 9(1)). If the feuduty is an unallocated *cumulo* (as often it will be) the superior must allocate the compensation in such manner as is reasonable, usually by following any existing apportionment (s 9(3)).

Once a notice has been served, the former vassal has 56 days to pay (s 8(5)). But if the amount due is £100 or more he can opt to pay in instalments (s 10). For instalment payments there is a one-off surcharge of 10%.

Unpaid compensation is not secured on the ground. Nor are arrears of feuduty (s 13(2)). So feuduty is taken out of conveyancing altogether. A person who buys property after the appointed day is not liable either for arrears or for unpaid compensation. So it will no longer be necessary to bother about feuduty redemption receipts.

As with the 1974 Act, the extinctive provisions apply also to other periodical payments, such as ground annual (s 54).

### Real burdens to go (up to a point)

The important subject of real burdens is dealt with in Part 4 of the Bill. The opening provision is s 16(1):

> Subject to sections 17, 18, 19, 22, 26, 27 and 58 of this Act—
>
> (a) a real burden which, immediately before the appointed day, is enforceable by, and only by, a superior shall on that day be extinguished; and
>
> (b) any other real burden shall, on and after that day, not be enforceable by a former superior.

So what is left? The answer is, quite a lot:

**Non-feudal burdens.** The Bill is confined to real burdens created in, or in association with (*eg* in a deed of conditions), a grant in feu. So burdens created in, or in association with, a *disposition*, are wholly unaffected.

**Rights of third parties.** Even within the class of feudal real burdens, only superiors lose their rights. If neighbours also have enforcement rights, these survive. So, for example, if a volume builder has feued a housing estate of 100 houses and given each house a right to enforce the burdens, the volume builder will, on the appointed day, lose its enforcement rights, but the burdens will continue to be enforceable by the owners of the 100 houses. All this makes it important to know, in particular cases, whether third party rights exist. If there are none, the land is free of the burdens, and the burdens can be deleted from the land certificate. Otherwise the burdens survive. The particular difficulty arises with implied enforcement rights, which can sometimes be hard to detect. The subject of implied rights is being tackled by the Scottish Law Commission in a separate exercise on the law of real burdens (see below).

**Facilities and services.** Burdens which regulate the maintenance, management, reinstatement or use of common facilities (*eg* a private road, or drainage system, or the common parts of a tenement, or a mutual wall) survive and are enforceable by the owners of those properties which take benefit from the facilities (s 22). The same is true of burdens regulating the provision of services. In most cases, of course, such burdens will already be enforceable by such properties, and would have survived feudal abolition even without express provision.

**Maritime burdens.** Sometimes, in feuing the foreshore or seabed, the Crown imposed real burdens. These are to continue to be enforceable by the Crown, notwithstanding the abolition of the feudal system (s 58).

**Neighbour burdens.** All the savings mentioned so far happen automatically, without the need for anyone to take any action. The final two savings require that the superior register a notice, in the statutory form, during the period between the coming into force of the provisions and the appointed day. Conveyancers who act for superiors should be consulting their clients, and, in appropriate cases, setting in train the necessary administrative arrangements. The provisions, however, are unlikely to come into force until 2001.

The more important of these savings is available if the superior owns land in the neighbourhood of the burdened land. This is governed by s 17. The idea is that, by registration of a notice, the right to enforce the burdens is transferred from the superiority to the neighbouring property. The burdens are thus converted from feudal burdens into neighbour burdens. A separate notice is required for each feu (though not for each burden) (s 40(3) and (4)). The notice must be registered both against the feu and also against the proposed benefited property. This is to achieve full transparency on the register.

Not all neighbouring land can be used for this purpose. A notice can be registered only if one of the conditions in s 17(7) is satisfied. The conditions are:

(a) That the land which by virtue of this section would become the dominant tenement has on it a permanent building which is in use wholly or mainly as a place of human—

    (i) habitation; or

    (ii) resort

and that building is, at some point, within one hundred metres (measuring along a horizontal plane) of the land which would be the servient tenement;

(b) that the real burden comprises—

    (i) a right to enter, or otherwise make use of, the servient tenement; or

    (ii) a right of pre-emption or of redemption; or

(c) that the land which by virtue of this section would become the dominant tenement comprises—

    (i) minerals; or

    (ii) salmon fishings or some other incorporeal property

and it is apparent from the terms of the real burden that it was created for the benefit of such land.

Of these (a) is much the most important. If the superior has a house or other permanent building which is lived in or otherwise used for people (and not just, *eg*, for storage), he can register a notice. But if he has only an empty field, he cannot. Sometimes, this will operate rather crudely. A superior who believes that, in his case, the rule is too rigid can apply to the Lands Tribunal, before the appointed day (s 19). The Tribunal is empowered to override the 100 metres rule if it is satisfied that, were the burden to be extinguished, there would be substantial loss or disadvantage to the superior as owner of the proposed dominant tenement. But before applying to the Lands Tribunal the superior must try to reach agreement with the vassal, under s 18.

**Conservation burdens.** There is one other case where real burdens can be saved by registered notice. Scottish Ministers are given power to draw up a list of conservation bodies (s 25). Any superior on that list can then preserve any real burdens which are conservation burdens, defined (s 26(2)) as burdens which have the purpose of preserving or protecting—

(a)  the architectural or historical characteristics of the land; or

(b)  any other special characteristics of the land (including, without prejudice to the generality of this paragraph, a special characteristic derived from the flora, fauna or general appearance of the land).

Once preserved in this way, the burdens are then enforceable by the former superior, now a conservation body. Note that there is no dominant tenement: in other words, a conservation burden is a real burden in favour of a person rather than in favour of land.

Finally, we should mention here that in one case compensation is potentially payable, but that this too requires the registration of a notice. Compensation is restricted to burdens which reserved development value to the superior (s 32). If a notice is registered, such burdens have a 20-year afterlife, beginning on the appointed day. If, during this period, the owner of the (formerly burdened) land breaches the (former) burden (s 34), he must pay the amount of development value so gained (s 36(1)), but this cannot exceed the amount by which the original consideration for the feu was reduced as a result of the imposition of the burden (s 36(2)).

## No leases of more than 175 years

As the law currently stands, no lease of a dwellinghouse can exceed 20 years (Land Tenure Reform (Scotland) Act 1974, ss 8–10), but the duration of other leases is not restricted. Section 65 of the Bill imposes a limitation on the duration of leases, of 175 years. This applies to new leases only and does not affect existing leases. The reason for the limitation is to avoid the creation of a pseudo-feudal system using leasehold tenure. No doubt there will be debate as to whether 175 years is the right figure, but the principle at least seems correct. Many other countries also have maximum periods for leases, for precisely the same reason.

## Miscellaneous reforms

The Bill removes from the statute book a great deal of feudal (and other) detritus. It repeals 45 Acts in full, as well as 246 sections and 57 schedules in other

Acts. Among the casualties are the kindly tenants of Lochmaben, tailzies, and thirlage.

## Report on real burdens

In anticipation of the abolition of the feudal system, the Scottish Law Commission has been working on a comprehensive reform of the law of real burdens. A lengthy discussion paper was put out for consultation in October 1998 (Scot. Law Com. DP No 106). A final report is expected during 2000. The Scottish Executive is already committed to introducing a bill based on the Commission's recommendations. The idea is that the bill—to be known as the Title Conditions (Scotland) Bill—should come into force on the same day as the feudal system is abolished.

# MISCELLANEOUS

### Leases, prescription, land registration, and *a non domino* titles

In *B G Hamilton Ltd* v *Ready Mixed Concrete (Scotland) Ltd* 1999 SLT 524 (OH) the defenders held a 999-year lease, created in 1891 and recorded in the GRS in 1895. The *dominium utile* was registered in the Land Register in 1985, and in 1997 was acquired by the pursuers, who duly completed title. However, in 1990 there had been an *a non domino* disposition in favour of the lessees. The Keeper registered them as proprietors with exclusion of indemnity. Although the wording is not central to the case, we give it for its interest:

> Indemnity is excluded in terms of Section 12(2) of the Land Registration (Scotland) Act 1979 in respect (1) that a Disposition to the Proprietors in Entry 1, of inter alia the subjects in this Title was registered on 19 Jan 1985 and ranks prior to the Disposition to the Proprietors in Entry 2, registered 26 Nov 1990 on which their entitlement was founded and also (2) that no evidence of Title prior to said Disposition to the Proprietors in Entry 2 has been produced to the Keeper.

The idea that two persons can be *simultaneously* on the register as owners (other than co-owners or joint owners) is strange. (See, further, an article by Professor Reid at 1991 *Juridical Review* 79.) Certainly there is nothing in the legislation which warrants an entry of this sort. Indeed, to the contrary, it is suggested that the legislation actually excludes any such possibility. For s 3 roundly declares that registration vests the interest (here, ownership) in the person registered. And it is simply not possible for two different persons both to be owners at one and the same time. (Other than as co-owners or joint owners, of course.) The word 'rank' which the Keeper uses betrays the truth. For ranking is possible only between *compatible* rights. For instance, two standard securities have a mutual ranking, precisely because one property can be subject to two standard securities. But two ownerships cannot rank with each other. If one ownership is superior to the other, the other is not merely *postponed*: it is *null*.

The Keeper's practice has, however, not yet been subject to judicial scrutiny: in the present case it was not a key issue.

Back to the story. In 1997 Ready Mix's name was (at their own request) removed from the register, leaving only that of the pursuers. The pursuers claimed that the *a non domino* disposition amounted to an implied renunciation of the lease. The action was dismissed. What had happened did not amount to an implied renunciation of the lease. Lord Hamilton:

> The recording or registration of an *a non domino* title is a mechanism not uncommonly used both innocently and properly where difficulties or ambiguities exist in a progress of titles. It does not, in my view, import the surrender of other rights in respect of the subjects, albeit the existence of an alternative basis for possession (as under a lease) may make it difficult to establish for the purposes of positive prescription that the possession is founded on the proprietorial title.

This is an interesting passage. We would like to comment on the last part of it. When there is a long lease and it appears that the landlord has disappeared from the scene it may be an attractive idea to turn the title into a property title by means of an *a non domino* conveyance. It is natural to suppose that if this is done and if the landlord does nothing for 10 years, then a prescriptive title will be established. But in fact the law is less than clear. The law of prescription requires that the 10 years of possession must be *founded on* the relevant deed. (Prescription and Limitation (Scotland) Act 1973 s 1.) In a case of this sort, it is arguable that the possession is not founded on the *a non domino* deed but is still founded on the lease. If that is right, after 10 years a good prescriptive title has still not been acquired. It is to this possibility that Lord Hamilton is referring. The law in such cases appears to be that if the rent is being paid then the possession is to be attributed to the lease but if it is not being paid it can be attributed to the other title: see David Johnston *Prescription and Limitation* (1999) para 16–27.